UPHOLSTERY

BASIC & TRADITIONAL TECHNIQUES

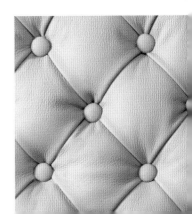

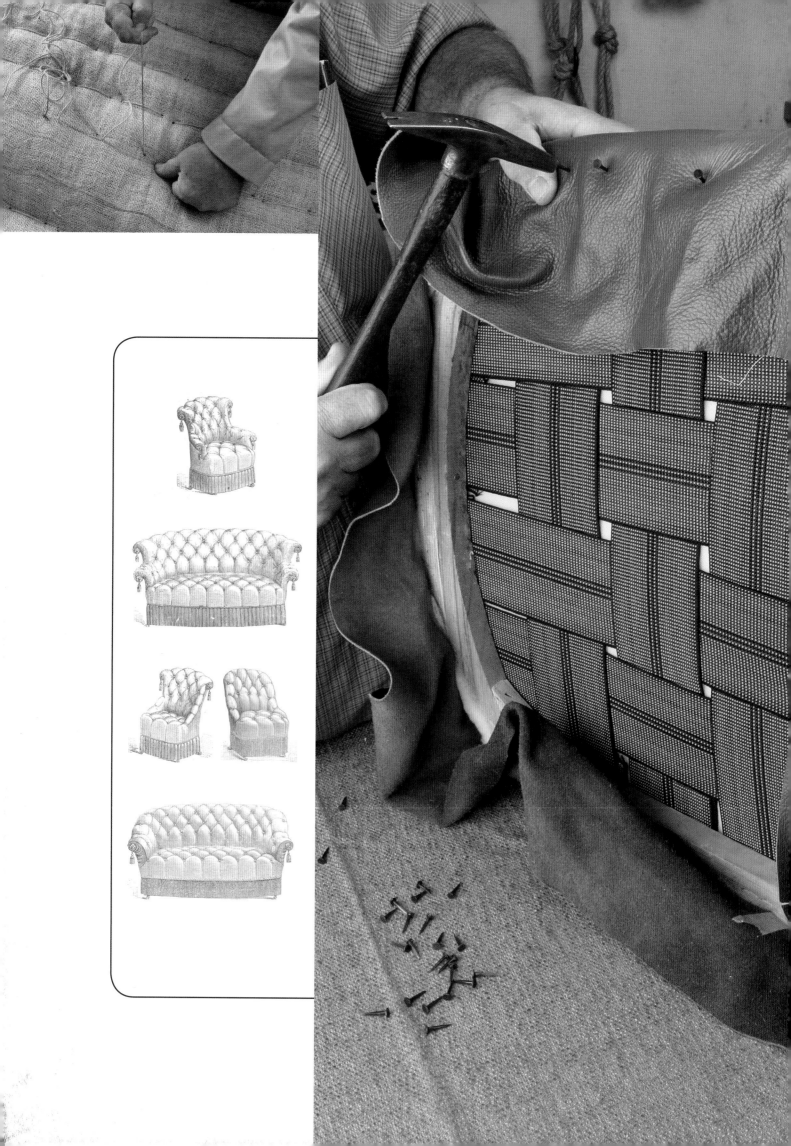

UPHOLSTERY

BASIC & TRADITIONAL TECHNIQUES

Santiago Pons

Eva Pascual

Jordi Pons

Mercè Garcinuño

4880 Lower Valley Road • Atglen, PA 19310

Library of Congress Control Number: 2015946645

Originally published as Tapiceriá by Parramón Paidotribo, Barcelona, Spain, © Parramón Paidotribo, 2013. Translated from the Spanish by Jonee Tiedemann.

Production Design by Danielle D. Farmer
Cover design by Molly Shields
Type set in Arial/NewBskvll BT/

ISBN: 978-0-7643-4855-6

Printed in China

Published by Schiffer Publishing, Ltd.
4880 Lower Valley Road
Atglen, PA 19310
Phone: (610) 593-1777; Fax: (610) 593-2002
E-mail: Info@schifferbooks.com

For our complete selection of fine books on this and related subjects, please visit our website at www.schifferbooks.com. You may also write for a free catalog.

This book may be purchased from the publisher. Please try your bookstore first.

We are always looking for people to write books on new and related subjects. If you have an idea for a book, please contact us at proposals@schifferbooks.com.

Schiffer Publishing's titles are available at special discounts for bulk purchases for sales promotions or premiums. Special editions, including personalized covers, corporate imprints, and excerpts can be created in large quantities for special needs. For more information, contact the publisher.

EDITORIAL: María Fernanda Canal; Editor: Tomàs Ubach; Assistant editor and image archive: Carmen Ramos; Coordination, texts and design: Eva Pascual i Miró, with Sofía Rodríguez Bernis in chapter "Brief History of Upholstery"; Technical consulting and realization of projects: Santiago Pons, Jordi Pons, Mercè Garcinuño in the chapter "Canework"; Collection design: Josep Guasch; Photography: Nos & Soto, archive Tapicería Pons, Ramon Manent (page 58); interior designs/styling, Lombardo y Decortex Firenze (pages 46 to 48);

DRAWINGS AND GRAPHICS: Farrés Il·editorial illustration; Layout: Estudi Guasch, S.L.

CON T

OTHER SCHIFFER BOOKS ON RELATED SUBJECTS:

Chinese Country Antiques: Vernacular Furniture and Accessories, c. 1780–1920, Andrea & Lynde McCormick, ISBN 978-0-7643-3314-9

Do-It-Yourself Tailored Slipcovers, Sophia Sevo, ISBN 978-0-7643-2972-2

Bespoke: Furniture from 101 International Artists, E. Ashley Rooney et al., ISBN 978-0-7643-4226-4

ENTS

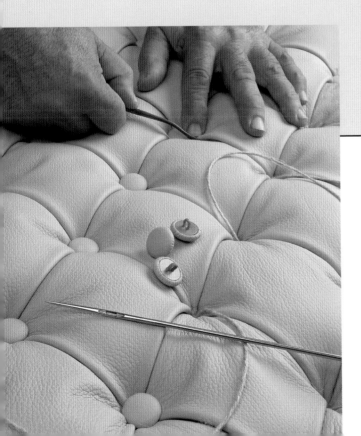

INTRODUCTION

Traditionally, upholstery has been considered to be a minor discipline among the crafts related to furniture, closer to decoration than to manufacturing. However, this is far from reality as upholstery is a craft on its own which contributes just like other related crafts to the creation of furniture and other items.

The craft uses proprietary techniques that require a comprehensive knowledge about related techniques, and the mastery of them is indispensable for carrying out any task. The technical aspects are essential; however, the aesthetic and decorative side is equally important.

The aspects that add environmental sustainability to this activity should also be kept in mind. For example, the restoration of furniture and objects enables their continued use. And in traditional upholstery, traditional and natural materials are recycled and used for new upholstery (whenever possible). So upholstering becomes relevant in terms of today's environmental consciousness.

This book presents traditional techniques of upholstery as well as the latest methods, and offers a complete panorama of the craft. The first chapter recounts a brief history of upholstered furniture. The second chapter presents the main materials and tools of upholstery. The third chapter, "Technical Processes," is divided into sections. We look at the considerations which must be kept in mind before starting a project: the influence of the design of the piece of furniture on the processes related to making the upholstery. The basic structure of traditional upholstery and adequate planning of the traditional processes, to provide a guideline for the project, are explained. The main techniques are given, step by step, and also included are other techniques for making special items or making repairs. Finally, the fourth chapter consists of various step-by-step processes and methods, via five upholstering projects. These let you go into hands-on detail in practicing the basic techniques.

A photo gallery with a wide variety of international examples offers creative ideas. A glossary as well as a bibliography are included for readers who want to increase their knowledge.

This is not meant to be a definitive manual of upholstering, but an in-depth and clear presentation of traditional techniques that are still relevant today, including modern methods and canework. Special attention has been paid to aesthetic components and the decorative solutions offered by upholstering. The reader will encounter useful examples throughout to help perfect the skills needed for this craft, as well as resources to inspire his or her creativity.

Santiago Pons Ferrer is an upholsterer with over fifty years of experience. He was trained in Barcelona's most prestigious workshops and later founded the Taller de Tapicería Artesanal Pons in Barcelona. He has held the title of Master Craftsman of the Government of Catalonia (Maestro Artesano de la Generalitat de Catalunya) since 2007, in recognition of his professional mastery of the craft. He has taught upholstery classes for more than fifteen years at the main restoration schools of Catalonia.

Jordi Pons Cort is the son of Santiago Pons Ferrer, and today heads the upholstery workshop Taller de Tapicería Artesanal Pons in Barcelona. He has worked there for thirty years, and combines traditional craft techniques with new and innovative methods, constantly searching for high-quality materials to perform both kinds of work. The workshop does restoration of upholstery for institutions, antique shops, and private individuals, as well as creating upholstery for interior outfitters and designers.

Mercè Garcinuño Garcinuño is a specialist in canework as it is applied to furniture, and has more than ten years of professional experience. She regularly collaborates with the Pons upholstery workshop, both in restoring antique furniture and in the creation of contemporary pieces.

Eva Pascual i Miró is a licensed art historian and specializes in museography and design and in preventive conservation. Her professional trajectory has taken her to various museums and cultural institutions throughout Catalonia, where she has documented furniture collections and decorative art; she has also worked as a manager of collections and as an exhibition coordinator, and has written numerous articles about decorative arts and Catalonian medieval furniture. She works with several publications, and is a member of the editorial staff of *Estudi del Moble (Furniture Studies)* magazine.

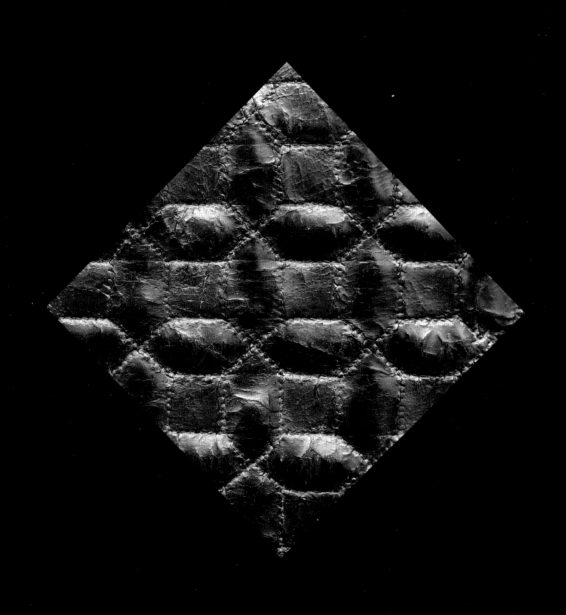

Upholstered
FURNITURE

Furniture has always been associated with upholstery—especially such items related to rest and comfort, including armchairs and beds.

However, there are many objects that apparently do not require it but which nevertheless have been adorned or complemented with fabrics: tables covered with tablecloths, trays which present items on top of some sort of cloth lining, libraries where the books are protected from dust with curtains...

It is almost impossible to imagine fabric-naked interiors of houses. Depending on the resources and creativity of the owner, the floor, walls, bedrooms, and even ceilings have for centuries been adorned with carpets, tapestries, cloths, and trims.

Fabric's function is not only ornamental; it isolates from cold and heat, protects the walls from damage, and provides visual and tactile textures which make life more comfortable. Since ancient times it has introduced comfort to dwellings. Fabrics can be made in a thousand different ways to adapt them to the furniture: from the simple edging bordering the fabric of medieval thrones, to the very elaborate tufting of furniture of the 19th century.

Brief history of upholstery

Traditionally, fabrics for domestic use were made on domestic looms. Contrary to this production based on a very simple economy, the manufacturing of commercial fabrics developed techniques and specific decorations which raised the cost considerably.

The Middle Ages

This fact became particularly evident during the Middle Ages, when the conquering of distances and means of communication made Oriental carpets and the products of the looms in Persia, Byzantium, and Cordoba absolutely extraordinary. Western monarchs and noblemen had a great desire for them, and paid enormous sums to hang them from their walls. Richly adorned fabrics also decorated furniture, often covering it completely, and the coverings' value and rarity made them more valuable than the covered furniture itself, crafted from local woods which were easy to obtain.

These luxury fabrics were so extraordinary and valuable that symbolic and ideological values were attributed to them, some of them of religious and liturgical nature. Others were emblematic and associated with the monarchy and the

honor it represented. This resulted in ecclesiastical hierarchies, led by the pope and bishops, covering themselves in white fabrics around the 3rd century to separate their bodies from the environment and to sacrify themselves. The holy character of the monarchs, God's representatives on Earth, was expressed early on by using fabrics that covered the thrones. They can be appreciated in the examples of the Byzantine emperors, and, imitating them, the European kings. The pulvinus, a classic cushion, is also associated with power: it flanks the seats and supports the feet, with the same significance of the footstools mentioned in the Bible, which symbolize the earth and the enemies over which Yahweh and the Jewish kings reigned: "The sky is my throne and the earth is the footstool of my feet" (Acts 7:49). Curtains in churches separated the space reserved for God from the believers. In the royal medieval halls, the emperors and the kings used them to separate themselves from their subjects.

Perhaps the baldachin, the transposition of the celestial realm where divinity resides, is the most characteristic textile element of the Middle Ages. It covered the seats of

▲ Armchair, second half of the 16th century. Museo Nacional de Artes Decorativas, Madrid, Spain.

honor and beds. Paintings show hundreds of representations which range from simple folded fabrics precariously hung from the ceiling, to the most exquisite examples with much decoration and suspended from wooden or metal frames.

Until quite recently there was no separation between public life, which was characterized by gestures and movements that expressed dignity and severity, and private life, where the attitude was free and relaxed and without any solemnity. These differences did not exist in the furniture of the Middle Ages. There was no room for intimacy. The bedroom was almost as public a space as the salon: people were received here, and the ceremonies for going to bed and getting up expressed the dignity of the most powerful.

The famous ceremony surrounding Louis XIV's rise from bed each day is the epitome of these rites. The bed had to be richly adorned. As in a theater, the king was the main actor and the courtesans were the public. Everyone who was conscious about his importance ended up imitating this scenery.

Even during the 16th century, a French magistrate would receive a peasant while reclining on his bed to consider the plea. The peasant man, certainly unaware of the secrets surrounding the powerful, may have thought that a fortuitious confusion offered

▼ Banquet at the court of Juan de Portugal. Jean de Wavrin, *Crónicas de Inglaterra*, 15th century, Brussels, Belgium.

him a gallant adventure. Encouraged by the high-pitched voice of the judge he may have tried to get into bed with him, most likely followed by detrimental consequences for him once the situation was clarified.

These beds were laden with mattresses and cushions and covered with richly adorned bedspreads. Until the mid-14th century they were used in layers, with one over the cushions and another over the bed cover, so that the contrast between the colors and motifs augmented the effect.

This combination was possible due to the bed's structure; it was made from a base with turned posts at the corners. These beds were adorned with simple curtains which were suspended to create a close cubicle against the wall. The beds, which consisted of a baldachin, canopy, and curtains affixed to a frame, which was hanging over the structure suspended by cords, are typical of the late Middle Ages.

Textile furnishings were particularly abundant because they were easy to transport. In times where the government of the royal and noble holdings required their physical presence, the courts were traveling ones. Furniture that could be taken apart—particularly seating furniture—and the light and adaptable fabrics converted any residence into an adequate living space, and made up the bulk of the baggage that continuously traveled through medieval Europe.

▲ Death of Maria of Austria. Juan de la Palma, *Vida de la Infanta sor Margarita de la Cruz*, Madrid, 1636. Bed with canopy, baldachin, and curtains typical of the 16th century.

◀ Back rest of padded leather seat, early 17th century. Museo Nacional de Artes Decorativas, Madrid, Spain.

Renaissance and Baroque

The long journeys and constant travel of sovereigns continued during the 16th century, but they started to diminish and eventually disappeared when the courts began to set up their residences in the capital cities. This development prompted the creation of more solid, stable furniture. The seats are the furniture elements which show this process of structural improvement most clearly, and as a secondary effect the filling or padding was developed. At first, folding seats stayed prominent, although they changed shape. The courtly paintings of Antonio Moro or Sanchez Coello show the protagonists reclining or sitting on *armchairs* fitted with seats and back rests. They consisted of leather or fabric rectangles reinforced from the bottom with nailed leather and straps which compensated for their fragility, with decorative tacks on the back rest frame and the lateral crossbeams of the seat. The horizontal jambs at the front and back had to be folded or removed in order to fold the seat like an accordion and allow its transport. The back rests made from wood were affixed at the back of the structure whenever the carving or marquetry which adorned them was supposed to be visible.

Some of the most luxurious chairs were entirely covered with valuable fabrics. They were invented in 15th-century Italy and were imitated in the rest of the European courts. Perhaps the most well-known example is the painting of Queen Maria Tudor by Antonio Moro, but thanks to his inventory we know that Philip II owned one as well. When the monarch died they were already out of fashion in Spain, although countries like England which were closer to the decorative tradition reflect later examples.

The sedentarization of daily life brought forth chairs and rests with a fixed frame that the fabric decorations could be nailed to. Although some of them continued to be flat, such as the leather chairs of the 17th century known as "Portuguese chairs," most of them were *stuffed*, and the filling and padding of furniture has characterized the history of furniture ever since.

This is a direct consequence of the quest for comfort that has characterized the relaxed family life of middle-class societies, which were not subject to the stiffness of ceremonial power.

The first attempts at filling were padded chairs that appeared during the last third of the 16th century. The seats and back rests

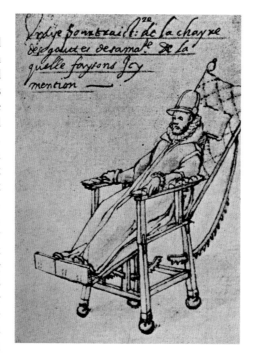
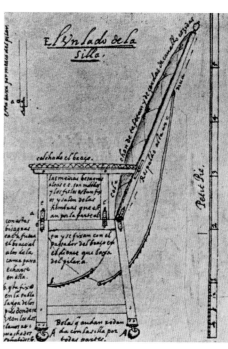

▲ Jehan de l'Hermite, seat of Philip II, *Le passetemps,* end of the 16th century.
The description of the seat shows that both the back rest and the arm rests are padded.

were filled with thin layers of horsehair or plant fibers, which were backstitched with various motifs such as crosses or diamondic patterns. The seat of Philip II, of which only a drawing is preserved, may be the most well-known example.

Nevertheless, upholstery as we understand it today made its appearance with

▼ Podium chair, mid 17th century. Museo Nacional de Artes Decorativas, Madrid, Spain.

the *"garniture à pelote"* (there is a proclivity to utilize the French term), which was bulky and affixed to wooden frames that formed the structure of seating furniture. The first models date back to the late 16th and early 17th century when the chairs featured a base made from a wooden board, which could be covered with a large quantity of filling, and which looked rather domed and fluffy with a fabric cover. We don't know when the filling began being mounted on straps affixed to a frame, a more flexible and elastic system than the board. One can assume that it was around the end of the 16th century. On the other hand we do know that during the last third of that century, cots with cotton straps to support the mattress were being imported from China, so that may be the origin of this development.

Little by little the back and arm rests became padded; they appear in the inventories of around 1640. The *modern armchair* was born, with a comfort potential which would determine its evolution into the 19th century.

When was the *chaise longue* invented? France claims its invention. But its early presence as Oriental cots in Spain presents another hypothesis. The Spanish documentation mentions "comfortable chairs in the manner of cots" toward the end of the Renaissance, perhaps derived from the luxury furniture from the Far Orient which was complemented with cushions and mattresses.

They were placed in the drawing room and the most intimate rooms of the house where parties and balls were held. The novels of Maria de Zayas describe these parties for us, where chocolate was served, conversations were held, stories were told, and sometimes there was even dancing. None of these cots has been preserved, but they must have been very luxurious and exclusive. And it makes sense to think it was those which gave origin to the French *couchettes* and the English *couches*, predecessors of the chaise longue, which were introduced at the beginning of the 17th century. And perhaps they were a development of the cots which diplomats and the numerous Spanish princesses and marriageable women took with them in their dowries to foreign lands. There is some evidence that supports this

speculation: for example, in a comedy by the Englishman John Fletcher (1624), the "Duke of Medina" has one of these pieces of furniture sent to the protagonist. It was in Europe where the modern techniques of filling transformed them, and where they evolved until they turned into the chaise longues that were introduced to Spain by the Bourbons in the 18th century.

The sofa is a European creation from between 1620 or 1630, probably resulting from adding a padded back rest to the cots. France and England dispute the paternity of this piece of furniture which was also known as a *canapé* and which was not entirely formulated until the last decade of the 18th century. At that point it became part of a set of furniture which has had a long history: a set of French origin, consisting of one or two canapés, various armchairs, and many chairs and stools, which would be the protagonists in the rooms of the 18th century.

The *estrado*, a Spanish custom inherited from the Moors, was a raised wooden platform in a corner of a room, used by ladies for receiving visitors. These consisted basically of fabric decorations, yet another example of the search for comfort by using fabrics. The estrado is an exclusively Spanish solution to furnish a lady's rooms. Originally from the medieval period, it lasted until it was replaced by French furniture well into the 18th century. It consisted of a platform made from wood or cork, and covered with Spanish, Turkish, Egyptian, and Berber carpets during winter, often overlapped one over the other; during summer it was covered with mats. The estrado contained large cushions with their top sides made from more valuable materials than the bottom sides which had to resist friction. The fabrics were perfectly displayed this way.

▲ Pedro Berruguete, *The Virgin's Suitors,* Walls of Nava (Palencia), around 1480. Note that the only furnishing consists of the estrado and one cushion.

▲ Diego Velázquez, detail of *Portrait of Philip the Prosperous,* 1659, with an upholstered armchair.

Although beds continued to be furnished with expensive fabrics, they were increasingly replaced by wooden frames. The baldachins and curtains were integrated into column structures, headboards, and frames with their own decoration, and tended to be folded into complicated draperies which evoked those of clothing as the 17th century progressed. When the potentates left behind their migratory lifestyle, the ornaments also became more stable, and were mounted on frames which were fitted to the precise dimensions of the various rooms. They were either lightweight for summer or more warm and insulating for winter. The baldachins were disappearing more and more, except for the royal palaces (where they are still in use today) and in nations where the stately aristocracy still reigned heavily, such as Spain or Sweden.

▲ Sofa, París, around 1715, with upholstery of the 19th century. Museo Nacional de Artes Decorativas, Madrid, Spain.

The 18th century

Little by little, social relationships had changed: around 1700 the relaxed, amiable, and intimate lifestyle had made inroads on the rigid norms of behavior derived from stately honor. Both in houses and in palaces, the family's center shifted toward other rooms like the study, where the social interaction became more relaxed and independent from traditional etiquette. The new attitude required new furniture, and much of it resulted in an unprecedented development of upholstery and fillings. Fashion trends accelerated and changed while the techniques for fillings and padding evolved at the same pace and rhythm.

France was leading this process. The reign of Louis XIV brought the domed seats and rests of the "goutte-de-suif." This was accomplished by affixing a web of plant fibers to the upper section of the seat's frame, usually consisting of esparto grass or hemp, the latter being more durable due to the length of its fibers. They were mounted either contiguously or separated by the same distance as that between the webbing. They were directly tacked to the wood, with a simple or double fold. The reinforcing fabric (the "toile forte" of the French upholsterers) extended across the webbing to improve durability and to keep the filling, made from coarse linen or from linen husk fibers, from becoming loose. This base was used to put on the filling, ideally from horsehair, but more often than not from plant material. It was finished with cover fabric ("toile de rembourrure") which maintained the shape of the filling, basted to the lower layers; the basting of the central area is rather developed, while the perimeter stitches are smaller to provide the exterior profile.

▲ Padded armchair in *goutte-de-suif*, first quarter of the 18th century. Museo Nacional de Artes Decorativas, Madrid, Spain.

◀ Armchair, Spain, last quarter of the 18th century. The domed seat is a model which appeared during the Rococo period. Museo Nacional de Artes Decorativas, Madrid, Spain.

◀ Office armchair, Madrid, early 19th century. Museo Nacional de Artes Decorativas, Madrid, Spain.

▶ Webbing of a Spanish seat from the late 18th century, nailed to the waist.

The monumental trapezoid seats and high square back rests of the first years of the century still imposed an erect and solemn posture. The French Regency and the Rococo periods, however, preferred curved profiles, low back and arm rests, and contoured shapes which allowed for a more relaxed and seductive position. The seats "en cabriolé" appeared, with an arched back rest, which were used for the environs where social life flourished, keeping those with a straight back rest reserved for ceremonial rooms. The former were called "courants" and the latter "meublants" due to their functions.

To create a more voluptuous and relaxed form, padded rims were introduced to raise the profile of the upholstery. The basting stitches became increasingly more complex, and those of the perimeter which provided shape and stability became shorter. At the same time it became popular to introduce a cushion to the central section of the arm rest. Also, many pieces of furniture had their feet shortened, and adopted curved lines, so the user could extend the legs, relax the hips and shoulders, and bend the arms, which were now free to move around and add gestures to the conversation. The most comfortable models were called "bergères" in French.

With the 18th century came the English-style chairs with carved back rests and a central brace, which became popular around the 1820s. Only the seat was upholstered, and they were composed of an independent frame which could be extracted to facilitate the change of the fabric. They were quite adequate for dining rooms, which were becoming a fixture of homes—earlier, meals had been served in the hall or the bedroom—where there was a higher risk of staining the furniture. Although it did not renounce the natural, more relaxed style, the advent of Neoclassicism and the return to reason favored elegant and courteous manners. For this reason, the shape of the seats returned to the straight and slender lines and this also transformed the fillings. They became higher to stylize the posture, with angular edges, independent of the square, rounded, or oval shape of the back rests or seats.

Although apparently simple, the configuration required an ever-increasing skill to stitch the supporting bastes, which varied depending on how they were placed, at the edges or at the center of the seat. This modality had its origin in England during the Rococo period, and was also adopted by France and all of Europe after 1770.

▼ English chair with biscuit seat. Spain, mid 18th century. Museo Nacional de Artes Decorativas, Madrid, Spain.

As the century advanced the variety of furniture with comfortable seats multiplied. They were mostly the work of the Parisian *menuisiers* (craftsmen in wood) who paid attention to fashion trends and who periodically updated their catalogs to increase sales. First the "duchesses" with curved shapes became very popular, as they allowed the ladies to recline when receiving visitors. During the Neoclassicism period they were replaced by the Greek "sultanas." A great number of sofas and couches were added. Kidney-shaped "à confidents," with small triangular seats added to the sides, had a lower back rest at one side, for sitting down in front of the chimney and letting the fire warm the feet. Others among the multitude, like the "paphose," were large and curved; one manufacturer of the time admitted that even he was not really clear about its characteristics. They all were test subjects for increasingly specialized upholsterers.

The beds continued to be dressed and adorned. The most novel bedcoverings were those made from light fabrics such as embroidered Chinese silk, stamped Indian cloth, and muslin (a fine cotton fabric). All of them permitted a graceful diagonal fall, so the large traditional columns were slimmed down or substituted with curved braces such as those of the "polonaise bed"; finally, Neoclassicism brought the fashion of the "imperials," very small baldachins which were opened like fans toward the edges of the bed. Other feminine furniture was adorned with similar fabrics, particularly as the dressing rooms became where the ladies received their friends and admirers in the morning.

▲ Crapaud armchair for children, Spain, mid 19th century. Museo Español de Artes Decorativas, Madrid, Spain.

The 19th century

This was the century of tufted upholstery. Although there had been previous attempts to find flexible and elastic solutions for seating furniture, it took until the 1830s when a model was presented at exhibitions such as those by Gillows and Dervilliers. It consisted of a base with coil springs. Under this base a waxed fabric was sometimes mounted to hide the webbing and a reinforcement fabric which was not essential. Another reinforcing fabric was placed on the coil springs, and on top of it the filling consisting of horsehair was mounted, the most common material until other materials such as wool, paper,

and, much later, foam padding appeared. Sometimes an additional top layer of down or feathers was added for comfort. Once the visible fabric was spread, stitches were made which penetrated the entire layer of the filling.

At the beginning of the 19th century the decorative fabric began to be folded so that the surface was shaped into small domes or cupolas. This gave the effect of a web of diamonds, which was decorated with buttons to cover the stitches on the surface. This is called tufting.

Tufting caused a radical transformation of seating furniture: it is the origin of comfortable seats, in which the wooden frame was reduced, sometimes so much that it was barely visible, leaving space for sculpted fabric shapes. Circular sofas took center stage in the halls; puffs were large stools where one or two persons could sit and recline; the "crapaud" chair was low and squat just like the toad which gave it its name; the Chesterfield sofa with its slightly everted arm and back rests and leather upholstery was popular in billiard salons and libraries.

The commercial catalogs of the large retailers lavished customers with variations of seats which were suggestively named "plush" and received terms such as Marie Antoinette, coussin, medicis, pompadour, lambrequin, ottoman, and more. The

◄ Filling from the 19th century with the webbing nailed to the bottom of the frame.

► Early tufted back rest, Spain, around 1845–1850. Museo Sierra Pambley, León, Spain.

▲ Tufted armchairs and wall ornament. A&L Streitenfeld, *Die Praxis des Tapezierers und Decorateurs*, Ch. Claessen et Cie., Berlin, Germany, around 1870.

for the vanguard of furniture. Seating furniture returned to open upholstery without filling, an expression of extreme formal simplicity. Simple flat-woven fabrics were utilized extensively, and some of the pioneers of modern furniture like Marcel Breuer, designer and professor of the Bauhaus school, started using synthetic fabrics toward the end of the 1930s. Consumer society witnessed the spread of synthetic foam which could be cut with industrial machines. But a good part of seating furniture continues to employ traditional techniques.

Sofía Rodríguez Bernis
Director of the Museo Nacional de
Artes Decorativas, Madrid

fashion of tufting also invaded the walls of restaurants, trains, the halls of transatlantic ships, and other public spaces which featured sumptuousness.

Fabrics of all kinds of textures, motifs, and colors were wildly mixed and took over the interiors of this time. But Modernism eliminated them, and looked for industrial alternatives to renew the textiles used

▼ Series of lambrequin seats, catalog of the Au Bon Marché shops, Paris, France, 1879–1880.

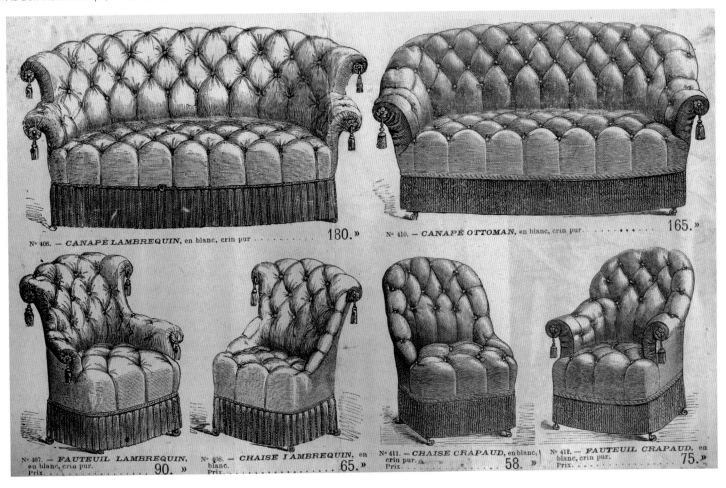

Nº 406. — CANAPÉ LAMBREQUIN, en blanc, crin pur . . . . 180.»

Nº 410. — CANAPÉ OTTOMAN, en blanc, crin pur. . . . . 165.»

Nº 407. — FAUTEUIL LAMBREQUIN, en blanc, crin pur. Prix . . . . 90. »

Nº 408. — CHAISE LAMBREQUIN, en blanc. Prix. . . . . . 65. »

Nº 411. — CHAISE CRAPAUD, en blanc, crin pur. Prix. . . . . 58. »

Nº 412. — FAUTEUIL CRAPAUD, en blanc, crin pur. Prix . . . . 75.»

MATERIALS
and Tools

This chapter presents the materials and tools used for upholstery, both traditional and the most innovative types. They have been grouped according to their uses, so you can easily find all of the tools and materials which are utilized for each technical process. You will also find explanations of their use, as well as practical tips.

This craft does not involve very specialized tools and materials; nevertheless, it is very important to know in detail both their characteristics and how to use them, in order to adequately and efficiently perform any part of the upholstery process.

We have also included the materials and tools required to perform canework, traditionally a craft related to basketmaking, but these days also used in upholstery shops. It has become another technique of the craft.

Materials

Webbing, springs, and fabrics

WEBBING

Consists of woven strips which are affixed to the structure or the frame, and form the base of the upholstery. There is a large variety of webbing made from different materials and of different widths, depending on the manufacturer; most have a width of between 2 and 4¾ inches (5 and 12 cm). They are usually made from jute or rubber-covered elastic. Rubber webbing is also manufactured, but its use is more limited.

Jute webbing can be purchased with fishbone weave or as flat-woven fabric. Elastic or rubberized webbing is available in different elasticities.

▼ Steel wire.

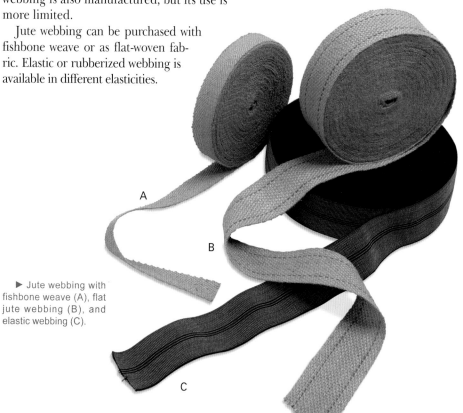

▶ Jute webbing with fishbone weave (A), flat jute webbing (B), and elastic webbing (C).

SPRINGS

Helicoidal springs are coil springs whose diameter is smaller at the center than it is at the ends, and are made from hardened steel.

They are flexible and return to their original position once the weight is lifted, which is why they are used in upholstery. There are various different types of springs, with different numbers of coils for different applications. Those used for the seat are made from thicker wire to provide a higher resistance, while those used for upholstering back and arm rests are thinner. There are also arched springs with a curved, ondulating profile, mainly used for seats.

WIRE

To create certain types of seats, like the comfortable seats, a frame must be made around the top section. Steel wire is used for this.

▼ Seat springs with four turns (A), five turns (B), six turns (C), seven turns (D), and seven turns with a higher strength than the previous (E).

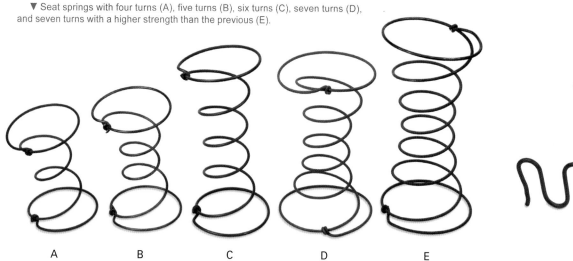

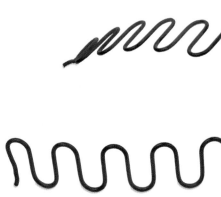

A   B   C   D   E

▼ Coffee bags.

▲ Burlap.

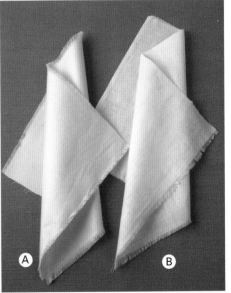

▲ Special fabric for down (A); muslin (B).

BURLAP

Also called hemp tow, this is used to cover the springs and the layer of horsehair for the filling of the upholstery. It is a very coarse fabric made from hemp fiber or jute (*Corchorus capsulares*, a plant from tropical regions). Burlap is available by the yard or in rolls. Coffee bags made of jute can be substituted for it; they are more economical, and are easy to obtain from importers or dealers specializing in coffee roasting.

MUSLIN

This is a thin, flat-weave cotton fabric which is used in traditional upholstery to cover the horsehair and the batting of the filling; it lies below the fabric or the covering leather.

SPECIAL FABRIC FOR DOWN

Making down cushions requires the use of a special down-proof ticking to prevent the down from perforating the fabric and sticking out. It is usually made from dense cotton with a high number of threads per square inch, typically a minimum of 180.

▼ Arched (zig-zag) springs.

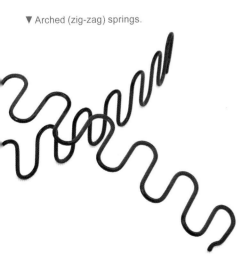

▼ Springs for back rests with four turns (A), five turns (B), and seven turns (C, D) which are mainly used for the low section of the rests.

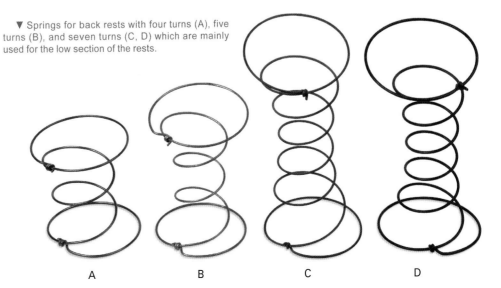

A   B   C   D

Affixing and sewing

JUTE SPRING TWINE

A thin string made from hemp that is used to tie and affix the springs of the upholstery. It is sold in rolls.

THREAD

In order to make ties and stitches a hemp thread is used, also called upholsterer's thread. It is sold in several gauges, depending on the manufacturer. The most commonly-used ones are medium-sized, composed of 4 threads. Waxed sewing thread is also available.

To make sturdy and firm stitches for fabrics at the rear sections, a jute thread is used. It is very strong and available in various colors.

Polyamide (polyester) thread (100%) is utilized for machine sewing the pieces of fabric that make up the final layer of upholstering

STAPLES

Today staples are used in place of tacks for numerous processes. A pneumatic or electric stapler allows for rapid work. There is a large variety of staples of different width and length (height), with the most commonly used ones being about half an inch (13 mm) wide. They are wide enough to affix different filling materials adequately, from fabric to other cover materials (leather, vinyl, etc.). Narrow staples can cause the ripping of the fabric when it is pulled taut.

It is best to have an ample selection of different sizes on hand, to be prepared for all kinds of tasks. Generally, staples with a shorter length (height) are used to staple to hardwoods, while longer ones ranging from 0.4 to 0.6 inches (12, 14, and 16 mm) are used for softwoods.

▶ Staples of 13 mm width (type 80/30): 4 mm (A), 6 mm (B), 8 mm (C), 10 mm (D), 12 mm (E), 14 mm (F) and 16 mm (G) height.

▲ Threads for use in sewing machine.

▲ Sewing thread (A), jute spring twine (B).

◀ Jute thread.

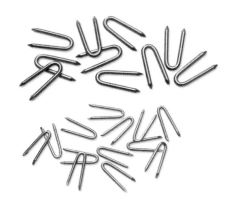

▲ Metal fasteners.

METAL FASTENERS

These are U-shaped zinc-coated steel pieces with sharpened points at both ends. They are used for upholstery to affix wire which makes up the frame of the comfort seats and for certain reinforcements of the back rests.

TACKS

These are short nails with a wide head. Tacks for affixing materials temporarily feature a square body and terminate in a very sharp point with a large head. The most appropriate tacks for upholstery are steel tacks with a small round body and a sharp tip. Compared to the former, they provide a more firm hold and do not tend to oxidize. Traditionally they were used to affix all sorts of materials, but today they have largely been replaced by staples. They are still used to affix the springs, and they are very suitable for areas where the stapler cannot reach, such as certain edges of chairs.

WHITE GLUE

White glue or carpenter's glue is a vinyl polyacetate, also called polyvinyl acetate or PVA. It can be dissolved by certain organic solvents and has great adhesive strength. It forms very flexible and resistant layers which are not affected by light and are not dissolved by certain products.

It is used for gluing wood and to affix the canework. It dries completely after 24 hours.

CONTACT GLUE

This glue is made from synthetic rubber (usually neoprene) with a solvent which hardens the glue as it evaporates. It has great strength and, once dry, is very resistant. It allows for instantaneous bonding. It does not allow for adjustments. Contact glue is applied onto the surface to be glued and allowed to dry for a few minutes until it is not sticky to the touch (this varies with the manufacturer).

Depending on the type, manufacturer, and the ambient conditions these glues can be worked between 5 and 15 minutes, during which the apparently dry glue layers can still be pressed together and bonded. They are used to affix foam and batting on wood or the webbing base.

There are also aerosol spray contact glues which are also composed of synthetic rubber. They are easy to work with, emit little odor, and are not harmful to the environment. They are applied some 6 to 8 inches (15 to 20 cm) apart and can be worked with for up to 30 minutes. They leave a transparent film. Some types have a regulator at the tip which allows for a precise control of the desired amount onto the area to be glued.

▼ Liquid contact glue (A), white glue (B) and spray contact glue (C).

▼ ▶ Tacks for temporary affixing (A) and steel tacks numbers 12 (B) and 8 (C).

Filling

HORSEHAIR

This is the long hair from the horse's mane. Traditionally this hair, clean and carded, was used as filling during the upholstering process. However, nowadays plant fibers with similar properties and look are used almost exclusively. These fibers are derived mostly from coconut (the fruit) or some palm species. They are easier to obtain and less expensive than horsehair, and sold in bags of various sizes.

BATTING

This is a non-woven fabric of polyester fibers which is used as the final layer of upholstery filling. It is manufactured in densities of 100, 150, 200 and 300 g/m2, although they may vary depending on the manufacturer. The most common one used in the shop is of density 300. For upholstering, resin-coated padding is utilized, that is, padding where glue has been utilized during its manufacturing process. For cushions, padding without glue is utilized.

POLYURETHANE FOAM

This is a polyester foam which is utilized as filling for some upholstery work. It is manufactured in various densities, and

▲ Various types of polyurethane foam. High-density (HR) 30 (A), density 30 super hard (B), density 30 soft (C), density 30 hard (D), density 25 fireproof (E), density 20 hard (F), and density 25 hard (G).

▲ Batting.

various qualities: extra firm, firm, medium, soft, etc., depending on the manufacturer. In addition, high-density and fireproof foam with similar characteristics to that of latex is available. It is sold in slabs, although many suppliers cut the pieces to size for different uses.

▲ Coconut fiber filling.

▲ Horsehair filling.

▲ Palm fiber filling.

▲ Fiber fill.

▲ Piping (A) and wedges (B).

FEATHER/DOWN

Feathers and down are used exclusively for making cushions. Down is the highest-quality feather; it is extracted from the neck and breast of geese and ducks, and consists of a core with thousands of filaments shaped like a star. Feathers and downs can be purchased in various qualities, from the smallest ones to larger ones, and they also can be purchased mixed with shavings and small pieces of polyurethane foam, which lowers the cost.

FIBER FILL

This is used exclusively for making cushions and consists of small bits of polyester.

WEDGES

These are pieces of chipfoam of different profiles, used for filling and to replace the task of sewing edges. They are available in various sizes and shapes for seat rests.

▲ Feathers.

▲ Mix of feathers and down.

▲ Mix of feathers with shavings and pieces of polyurethane foam.

Finishing

TRIMS

Trims are used to finish upholstery by covering unions between the cover and the structure. They add an interesting decorative element which both highlights the character of the upholstery, and entirely changes the final look. Trims come in different forms, cords, braids, or tassels, and are usually purchased ready to be applied. Cords are round and/or plaited. Braids are bands which can be flat or chain-shaped. The latter can be affixed to the upholstery with special thin tacks with small heads which are almost invisible once they are inserted. However, these days all trims can be affixed with hot glue.

▶ Braids.

▲ Tassels.

▲ Nails for braids.

◀ A selection of cords.

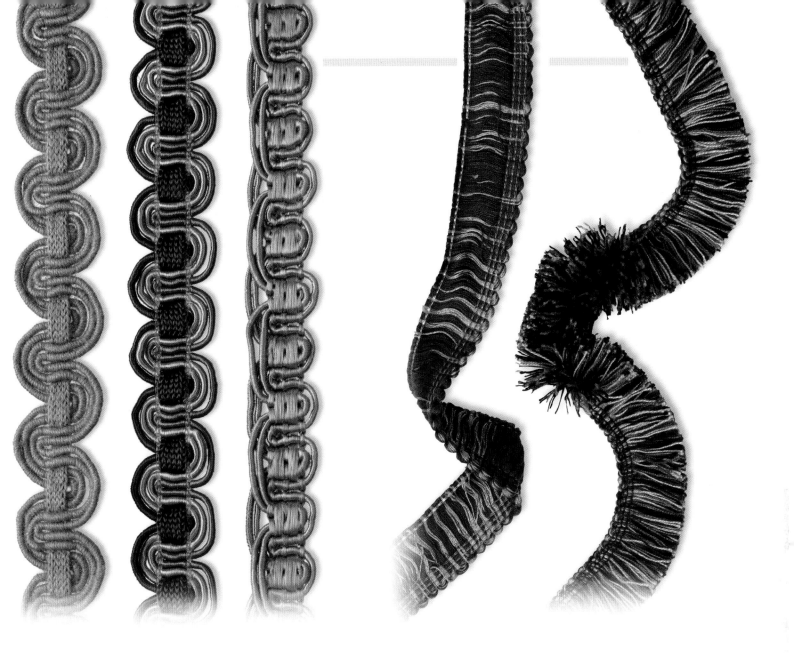

▲ Braids.

▲ Fringe bands. They are purchased with the lower section sewn, and they are unstitched once they have been affixed to the upholstery to achieve the fringe look.

▼ Fringes.

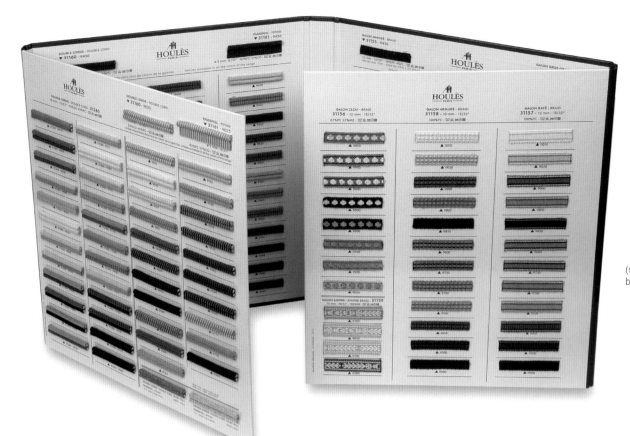

◄ Samples of piping (simple and double) and braids.

◄ Cores for piping: braided (A) of high quality, and rope (B), of lower quality than the braided version.

PIPING OR WELT CORD

This is a hem with a round profile. It can be made in the shop using a core and wrapping it with the desired cover to match the upholstery, or can be purchased ready for use.

BUTTONS

Buttons can be made in the shop. They consist of a metal or plastic base with a ring, which is used to sew them to the upholstery, and of a top metal section which is covered with the selected material.

GROMMETS/VENTILATORS

Circular metal pieces similar to rings, they are used for cushions covered with leather or vinyl/synthetic leather to allow for the air inside to escape when the cushion is pressed; this prevents the seams or the leather from ripping.

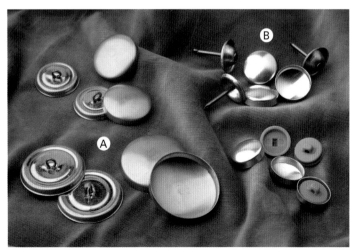

◄ Buttons (A) and nails with shells (B) to cover with fabric.

▼ Grommets.

NAILS

Decorative nails can be used for finishing upholstery. These are short nails with large heads, either flat or domed. There is a large variety of nails with many different profiles, shapes and types of finish. Choose the ones most appropriate for each task. They can also be created in the shop, covering the heads with the covering material most appropriate for the work to be done.

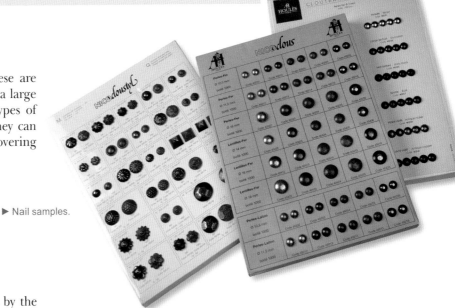

► Nail samples.

Lining

FABRICS

The final look of a piece of furniture is largely determined by the type and characteristics of the fabrics and the trims. Traditional upholstery involves a large number of technical processes which do have an impact on the final result, but the look is mostly due to the fabric, as it is the most important visual element. It is essential to choose the right covering for each project: fabrics, leather, or synthetic materials.

A wide variety of fabrics is suitable for upholstery, made from very different materials. Some of them can be very expensive, another reason to choose the fabric which is most suitable for the task. In all cases, a strong fabric must be chosen—one which does not rip easily and is sturdy enough to withstand tension. The choice also depends on the intended use of the furniture, its style, and where it will be located. In addition, decorative elements of the fabric such as color, sheen, and texture must be considered.

► Samples of fabrics for upholstery.

To mark fabrics for cutting, tailor's chalk is utilized. It marks the cutting lines at the rear side without staining it and it does not leave behind dust.

◄ Samples of fabrics for upholstery.

LEATHER

Leather can be used for lining. The highest quality leather is full-grain leather (dermis) with a visible texture of pores on its surface. Each type of leather features a specific grain pattern depending on the animal it came from. Cow leather is most commonly used for upholstery although other types of leather may be utilized. Tanned leather with fur can also be used. A large variety of qualities and finishes is available, of many colors and textures. Some of them have a fireproof finish or they are treated to be resistant against dirt and stains. These two finishes are also applied to fabrics.

SYNTHETIC MATERIALS

They are made from artificial materials which imitate the look and feel of leather or which have a surface with a plastic appearance. Those which are made to imitate leather are also called faux leather and consist of PVC or PU, the latter being more flexible and resistant than the first. Fabrics with a plastic covering provide a wide variety of colors and finishing and are usually made from PVC.

Generally, if these materials are of good quality they are resistant to wear and tear; their colors are light-resistant and they stay in good condition for a long time.

▼ The fabrics are marked with tailor's chalk before cutting.

◄ Samples of leather for upholstery.

► Samples of some synthetic materials: imitation suede, microfiber of 60% polyamide and 40% polyurethane.

Caning

CANE

Cane seats are made from rattan. It is a tropical plant with the characteristics of palm trees and lianas (*Calamus rotang* and other species) which grow rapidly and feature very long stems, up to 3 feet long. The bark and the core are mechanically extracted.

The bark of the stem is used for caning. It is very flexible and strong, and is available in various widths, the most common ones being between 1.8 and 2.5 mm.

BINDER CANE

The inner core of the rattan stem, called reed, is cylindrical, smooth, long, and knot-free. It is very porous and flexible, easy to bend and to work with, and is used to bind, or finish, the seat edges. Binder cane is sold in different thicknesses, commonly ranging from 4 mm to 6 mm.

MACHINE-WOVEN CANE WEBBING

Ready-made cane webbing is also available. It is used on seats that have a groove cut around the perimeter, and is held in place with reed spline. It can be useful for seats that don't require traditional, hole-to-hole caning.

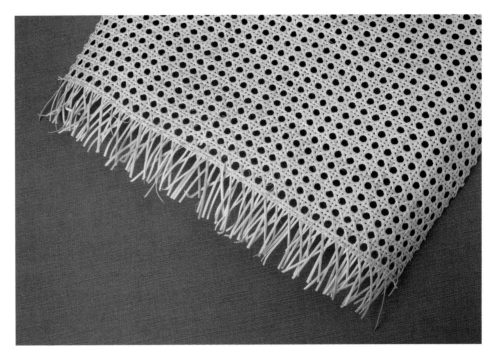

▲ Machine-woven cane webbing.

▶ Binder cane, 4 mm thickness.

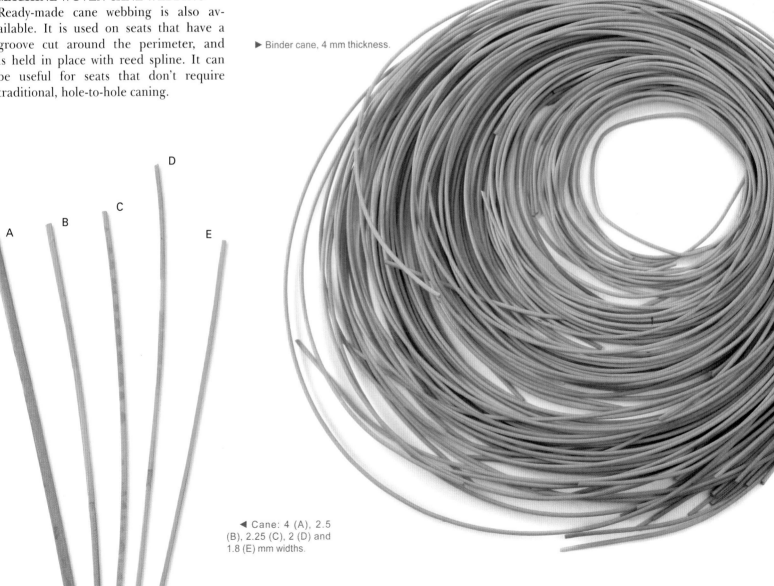

◀ Cane: 4 (A), 2.5 (B), 2.25 (C), 2 (D) and 1.8 (E) mm widths.

Tools

Cutting, extracting, and nailing

PLIERS
These are steel pliers with curved handles and square or conical tips which are used to cut or to bend wire. They can also be utilized to extract tacks or staples.

STAPLE LIFTER
This tool consists of a steel bar with a bent tip which is split and features a wooden grip at the other end. It is utilized to grab the head of the tacks and staples to remove them by leverage when existing upholstery must be removed.

PINCERS
A steel tool composed of two curved tips with a cutting edge. It is used both for extracting nails and staples and for cutting them.

MALLET
Wooden hammers with a wide and heavy head. They are mostly used to extract tacks and staples by hitting the grip of the staple lifter to apply more force.

RIPPING TOOLS
Used for stripping off tacks, staples, and fabric from furniture frames.

SCRAPER/PALETTE KNIFE
A tool consisting of a flat and thin metal sheet, wide and flexible and with a handle grip. It is used to strip frames or structures which need to be reupholstered, to remove remnants of glue, and to apply adhesive to large areas.

UPHOLSTERER'S HAMMER
A small and lightweight hammer with a small head used to nail tacks. One end of the head is flat and thinner at the end than it is at the center, while the other end is bent slightly downwards and split in a V shape. The first is used to nail tacks, and the other end is used to lift and extract them. Some models are magnetized to facilitate the work with tacks.

▼ Pliers (A), staple lifters (B), pincers (C), mallets (D), ripping tools (E), scrapers/palette knives (F), upholsterer's hammers (G), carpenter's hammer (H), razor knife (I), and scissors (J).

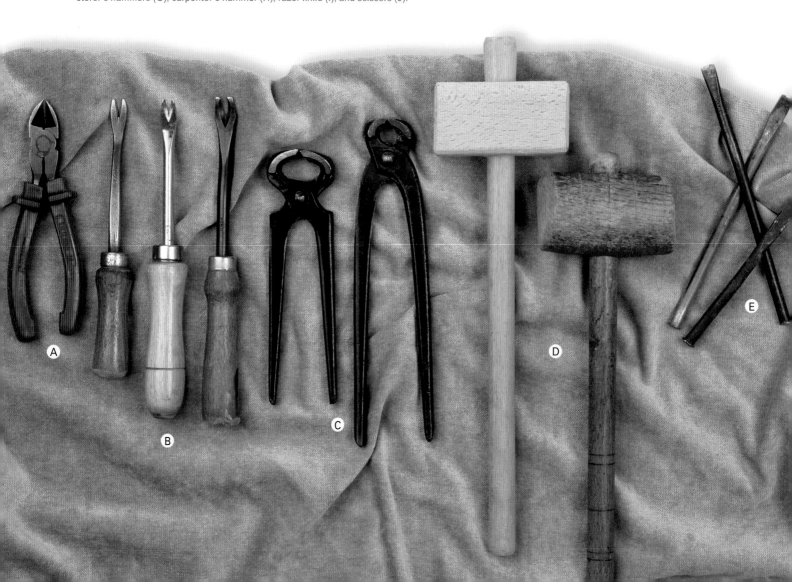

CARPENTER'S HAMMER

This hammer is heavier than the upholsterer's hammer and features a flat side and a downward curving side with a V-shaped cut. It is used for simple carpentry work, to nail and to remove nails.

RAZOR KNIFE

A knife with changeable blades featuring a flat grip, made from plastic or metal. The blade can be slid in and out to adjust its length. When the blade becomes blunt it can easily be clipped off, thanks to the scored lines, in order to continue with the unused section. It is used to make precision cuts.

SCISSORS

They are used to cut a wide variety of materials. Have several types of scissors and, whenever possible, use the same scissors to cut the same materials only. For scissors used on covering fabrics, especially, it is best not to use them for any other material.

PUNCHES

These are metal tools with a cylindrical shape at one end to make holes. The punch is used on leather and fabrics by placing it vertically onto the piece to be punched and hitting it on its opposite end with a hammer. It is mainly used to cut material for covering buttons.

▲ Hollow punches.

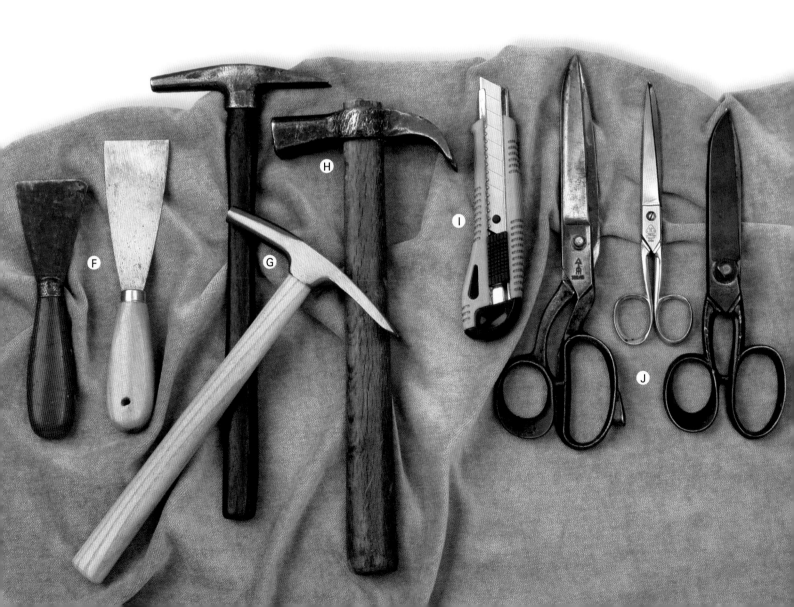

Sewing, affixing, adjusting, and applying

UPHOLSTERER'S NEEDLES / CURVED NEEDLES

They have a round profile and are shaped like a semicircle. They are used to sew springs and burlap as well as for making seals and reinforcements. They are sold in a large variety of sizes and qualities. Having a large selection in the shop allows you to choose the most appropriate for each task.

SURGICAL NEEDLES

They are made from stainless steel and are very useful for sewing upholstery leather. They are smaller than upholsterer's needles and feature a very sharp triangular tip which helps to perforate even the thickest leather with precision.

DOUBLE-POINTED NEEDLES

These are 7- to 15-inch-long (20 to 40 cm long) needles with double points, that is, they are pointed at both ends although only one end has an eye. They are used to sew the filling with a topstitch.

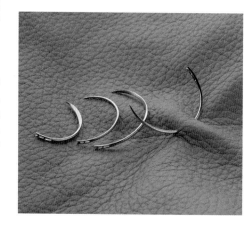

▶ Surgical needles.

PINS

They are used to hold fabrics in place while working.

SKEWERS

Large thick needles with a curved top end. They are used to temporarily affix the burlap, the covering, etc. They are sold in various sizes.

PUNCHES

Tools consisting of a very thin steel tip, with a handle. They are used to adjust horsehair filling.

▼ Upholsterer's needles (A), double-pointed needles (B), pins (C), skewers (D), punch (E), and regulators (F).

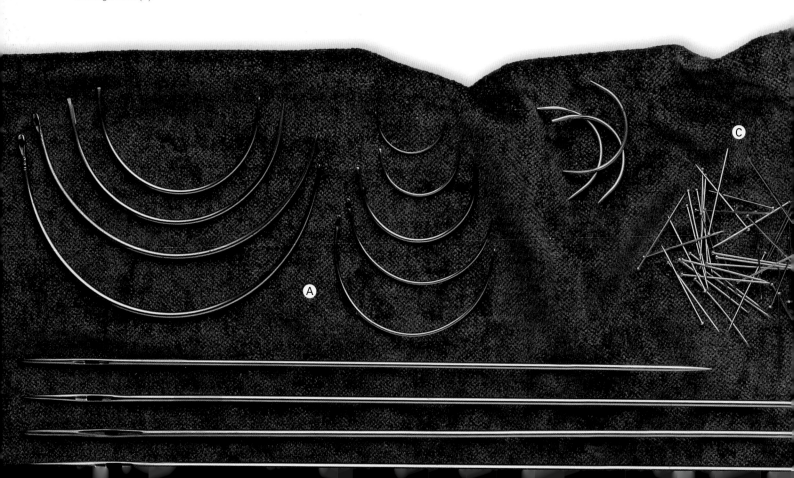

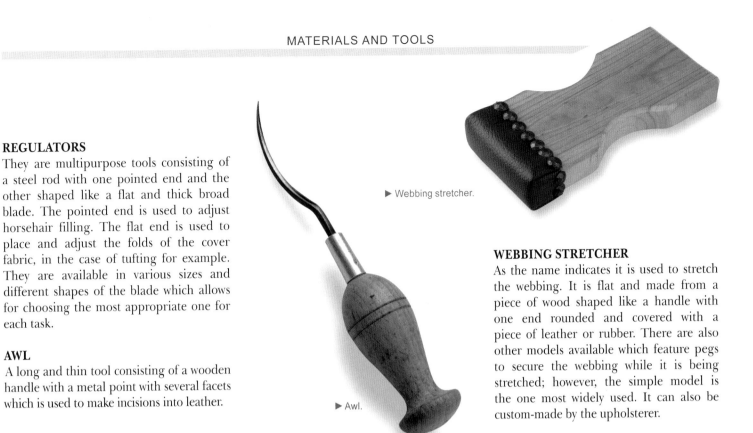

► Webbing stretcher.

► Awl.

REGULATORS

They are multipurpose tools consisting of a steel rod with one pointed end and the other shaped like a flat and thick broad blade. The pointed end is used to adjust horsehair filling. The flat end is used to place and adjust the folds of the cover fabric, in the case of tufting for example. They are available in various sizes and different shapes of the blade which allows for choosing the most appropriate one for each task.

AWL

A long and thin tool consisting of a wooden handle with a metal point with several facets which is used to make incisions into leather.

WEBBING STRETCHER

As the name indicates it is used to stretch the webbing. It is flat and made from a piece of wood shaped like a handle with one end rounded and covered with a piece of leather or rubber. There are also other models available which feature pegs to secure the webbing while it is being stretched; however, the simple model is the one most widely used. It can also be custom-made by the upholsterer.

Machines

BUTTON MACHINE

Used to cover buttons, it is a manual press firmly attached to a workbench with bolts. The base has a space with a spring or coil at the bottom where the molds for mounting the button are placed, and where the two sections which make up the button and the covering fabric are placed. The vertical axis also features a spring and a lever which is used to firmly press on the molds. This results in the lower section of the button being inserted into the upper section, which is lined on the outside.

GROMMET / BUTTONHOLE MACHINE

This is also a manual press, attached to the workbench. It features a tip to hold the grommet pieces, and is lowered onto the lower support where it is affixed. This press also works with other accessories such as punches for making holes.

▲ Buttonhole machine.

▲ Covered button dies of various sizes to cover buttons: top dies (A), bottom dies (B), and wooden plunger to insert the covering into the top mold (C).

STAPLER

Tacks have been replaced by staples to affix certain materials (mostly fabrics and batting) during the upholstering process. Pneumatic staplers allow for quick work and reduce the total project time considerably. They also allow for a reliable and durable attachment, without requiring a lot of strength. They are, though, fairly expensive, since a compressor must be used with the stapler to produce the compressed air for the gun. Various staplers can be connected to the same compressor using flexible hoses. Squeezing a trigger forces the staple into the material while reloading from the bottom section, which allows for effective and quick work. They can feature short or long noses, the latter being particularly useful for difficult-to-reach areas such as corners.

There are also electric staplers which are less expensive than pneumatic staplers. Some models feature rechargeable batteries so don't need to be connected to an electrical outlet. However, pneumatic staplers are better suited for professional shops or large projects. To mount springs it is more practical to utilize manual staplers.

◄ Grommet and buttonhole machine.

► Manual stapler.

▼ Compressor.

► Grommet dies and punches.

◀ ▼ Pneumatic staplers: long nose (A) and stapler with short nose (B).

◀ Electric stapler.

◀ Hot glue gun and glue sticks.

HOT GLUE GUN

A hot glue gun applies hot glue to attach trim when finishing the upholstery work. It allows for a simple and fast bond that is permanent. The glue comes in round sticks, which are placed into the nozzle on top of the gun and are heated and applied with the front tip of the gun. Most of the glue guns feature a lower support made of wire to allow for setting the gun down on the workbench. They usually heat up quickly (some 6 minutes) and maintain a constant temperature of around 392 °F. Some models feature a nozzle with a closing mechanism so that the glue does not drip when the gun is not in use. Hot glue dries rather quickly and, once applied, it is very strong and durable. The glue is transparent, thus very suitable for upholstery work.

SEWING MACHINE

An electric sewing machine is indispensable in the shop. It is used to make piping with the desired fabric, and to join fabrics, leather, or synthetic cover materials.

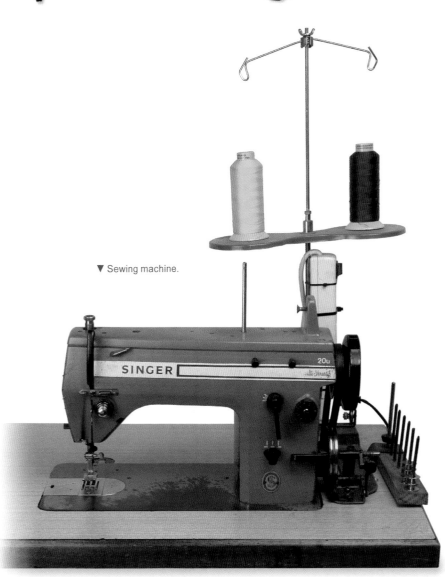

▼ Sewing machine.

Canework

HOOP
A long band of metal, usually iron, used to assist with making the cane webbing. It is very flexible and sturdy, and separates the vertical strands to facilitate the horizontal weaving. The hoop is also used to adjust the canes once they are woven, by tapping until they are aligned evenly and form cells.

TEES AND SUPPORTS
Golf tees are used in canework for tensioning and for the plaiting of the sewn cane webbing. They are very useful, with their tips which fit into the openings the canes pass through, and their top wider sections which provide a handle. Round iron rods can also be used as supports and to move the canes.

WEDGES
These are wooden triangular pieces with one very sharp angle. They are made in the workshop to fit the job's requirements, and are used to introduce the rattan core into the rabbet of the seat for setting and adjusting the canework.

CLAMPS
For canework, plastic clamps are used to hold the the project in the appropriate position while the glued cane is drying.

▶ Hoops and rod.

▼ Tees made from plastic (A) and wood (B).

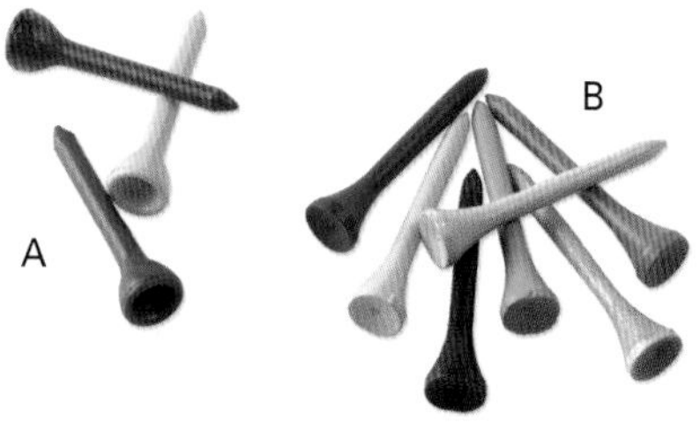

A

B

▶ Wood wedges made at the shop.

▲ Iron supports.

▶ Clamps.

ROTARY TOOL

This is a small electric tool with a drill chuck at the tip which can be fitted with a large variety of cutters, discs, and drills, among other things. The rotary tool turns at high speed and allows for quick high-precision work. It is used to remove binder cane remnants from canework, and glue remnants from the grooves of the furniture's frame. Rotary tools powered by rechargeable batteries are also available. Most feature a speed selector.

DRILL

This hand-held power tool is used to perforate various materials. It too can be utilized to remove glue remnants from holes and grooves. The accessories available make it a versatile tool that can be used for cleaning, sanding, drilling, etc.

SCREWDRIVER

A tool consisting, basically, of a steel rod with a tip that is shaped like the screw to be used with it. It is utilized not only to insert and remove screws, but also for inserting canes into the frame.

CUTTING PLIERS

Small cutting pliers are used to cut the canes and the binder canes, and are often used to cut wire and small metal pieces.

CHISEL

A chisel, usually between $3/16$ to $1\sqrt{3}{4}$ inches in length, is utilized to extract the cane from the furniture's rabbet.

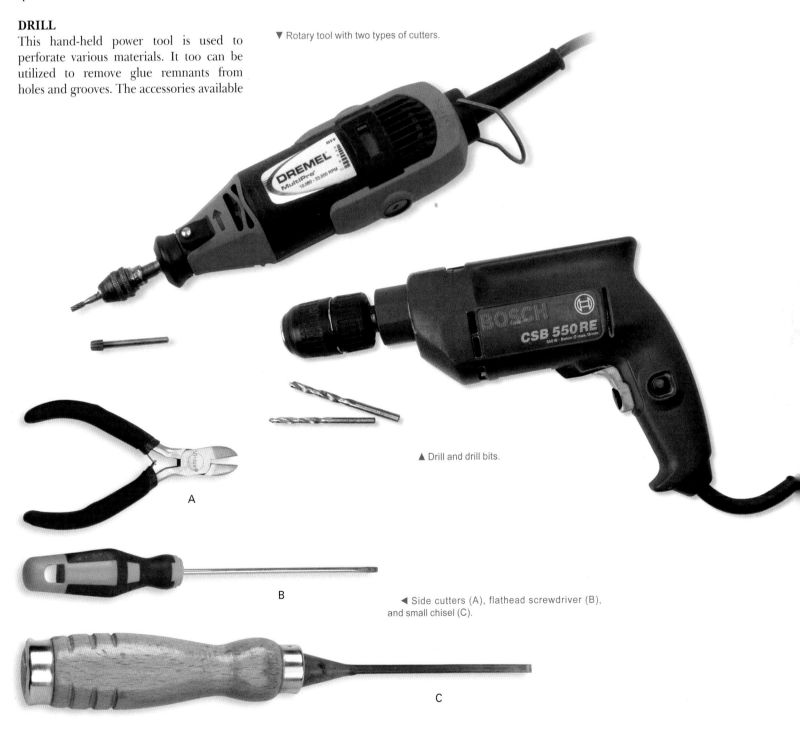

▼ Rotary tool with two types of cutters.

▲ Drill and drill bits.

◀ Side cutters (A), flathead screwdriver (B), and small chisel (C).

A

B

C

TECHNICAL Processes

Upholstery involves a significant number of technical processes, some of which are quite involved. This chapter is divided into four sections, to explain the processes in detail. The first section explains the foundational aspects, and shows the importance of considering the design of the piece of furniture or object. That has a direct impact on the upholstery techniques to use. The basic structure of traditional upholstery is also shown, including a guide for all of the processes involved. The second section explains in detail the basic techniques of traditional upholstery, including tufting or deep buttoning, so that anyone can learn to perform each task in the process. The third section presents some specialized techniques and processes for making special items and repairs. The last section is dedicated to canework.

Prior Considerations

Upholstery always involves a certain series of processes which are combined to perform the task, and which must be understood in detail. However, before starting any work, it is important to understand the design and elements of the item, since they determine the particulars of each task. Also, it is essential to understand the importance of correct planning and preparation.

◄ Wooden frame of an antique chair. The seat and the back rest will be in simple style.

▲ Wooden frame of an antique sofa. The seat will be fixed with springs and the back rest will be simple.

◄ Wooden frame of a contemporary armchair. The seat will be a webbed and spring seat.

► Basic structure of fixed seat without cushion on a contemporary ottoman.

The furniture: design

One of the essentials of this craft is to understand the importance of the design of the pieces of furniture that are to be upholstered.

The design of the piece, whether it is a new project or something already built, whether it is a prototype, part of a commercially-produced line, or a one-of-a-kind object, will influence the upholstery task: the type of upholstery and the processes required, the techniques and materials utilized. The design has a decisive influence on the final result.

The upholsterer must know the characteristics of the furniture and choose the most appropriate materials and processes. Antique furniture should be upholstered with materials similar to the original ones whenever possible, using traditional techniques. In the case of modern furniture, all depends on its particular characteristics. Choosing inadequate techniques and materials will invariably result in unsatisfying results, and may even render the furniture entirely unusable.

THE FRAME

The general characteristics of each piece of furniture are determined by the features of its frame. The frame makes up the skeleton of the piece of furniture and provides the support for the upholstery that will be mounted on it. The frame design will define the type of seat, back and arm rests for furniture that has these elements. Antique and modern furniture is made of wooden frames which often require a traditional upholstery job, although modern pieces may require a type of upholstery consisting of modern materials with modern processes, that is, synthetic materials with non-traditional techniques. Generally, modern-style furniture requires materials and techniques which are quicker to perform and less expensive, and adapted to the characteristics of its frame.

TYPES OF SEATS

As mentioned previously the type of frame will define the type of seat. In terms of upholstery, seats are a more complex part of the general structure of the piece of furniture, so it is important to know the different types.

► View of the basic frame of a coil spring seat. In this case the springs are affixed onto lower braces of the seat with fasteners and with a steel wire ring at the bottom section. The springs are perfectly aligned to the seat's frame and don't stick out.

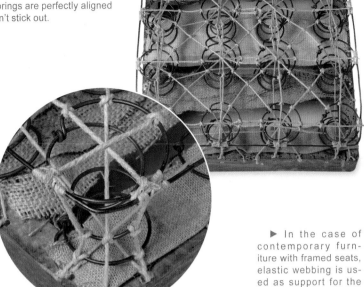

▲ In contemporary furniture, the polyurethane foam is affixed to the wooden frame and covered with batting.

► Detail of the tied springs at one of the corners. The type of seat determines the fastening of the springs, which are affixed at the top and at the two bottom rings.

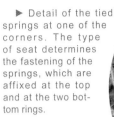

► In the case of contemporary furniture with framed seats, elastic webbing is used as support for the polyurethane foam.

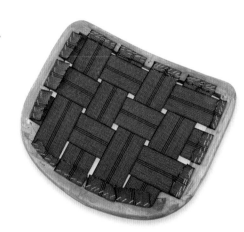

UPHOLSTERY

With regard to traditional upholstery using traditional techniques, the seats may be simple, fixed, or comfortable. Simple seats are the easiest, made using a base of webbing with filling and batting on top of the filling. This seat style is usually used for chairs for everyday use.

Fixed seats are the most common ones, both in antique and modern furniture. They are made with a webbing base on which the springs are affixed; these are in turn tied directly to the top structure of the seat so the seat is placed inside the frame. Fixed seats may or may not have a cushion. With a cushion, the total height of the upholstery, that is, the springs plus the filling and batting, is the correct height for sitting comfortably. Without a cushion, it is the frame and the general structure of the piece of furniture that

determines the positioning of the springs. These, together with the filling, need to be lower than normal in order to sit comfortably when a cushion is placed on top of the sprung seat.

In the case of comfort seats the springs are placed on the webbing, just as in fixed seats, however, those which make up the front line are affixed to the wooden structure with metal fasteners. In this case the mounting of the springs is different from the fixed seat's, more complex and complete, particularly at the front and the corners. Then the diagonal star-shaped ties are made. The result is a flatter seat than the fixed seat which moves independently from the frame when sitting on it. As with a fixed seat, it may or not feature a cushion depending on the frame design.

Contemporary or modern upholstery utilizes synthetic materials which require

only basic techniques. The seats may consist of a wooden base or other type of support on which the polyurethane foam is affixed with glue, and this is then covered with batting. Certain pieces of furniture that have a framed seat without support may require elastic webbing as the base for polyurethane foam, which is then covered with batting also.

CANEWORK

Seats made from cane can be woven, or can use machine-woven cane webbing. Woven canework is used on seats with hole-drilled frames used to thread the canes. Seats with machine-woven cane webbing require only a rabbet on the top of the frame, where the cane webbing is affixed, and which is later covered with binder cane.

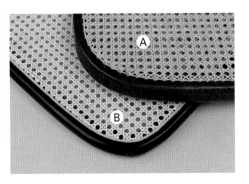

◄ Seats with woven cane (A) and with machine-woven cane webbing (B).

► Seat with canework (A), where the holes in the frame with the canes passing through them are visible, and a seat with machine-woven cane webbing (B) with a solid frame.

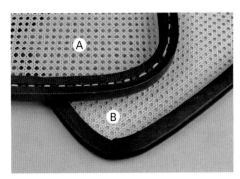

Structure of traditional upholstery

Traditional upholstery is a craft where various processes are used, and the finished work may appear very complex due to those various techniques; but when the general structure of upholstery is understood, all becomes much clearer. First it is important to analyze the design and the structure of the furniture piece, to plan the work. This includes the frame of the object to be upholstered, which, depending on its type, may consist of only the seat; seat and back rest; or the complete piece of furniture.

First, the webbing is placed and affixed, which provides the base for the springs. The springs are stitched to the webbing in three or four places around the bottom rung of each spring. Next, the springs are tied together with the 8-way tying technique using jute twine that is anchored on each seat rail with tacks.

Once the springs are compressed and secured with the spring tying, the first layer of burlap is placed on top. The top of the coil springs are stitched to the burlap using upholsterer's hand-sewing thread or twine. The burlap is then pulled and attached to the seat rails, front to back and side to side. This compresses and secures the springs even more.

Ties are made using twine that will hold the first filling in place. The filling is "teased" with a regulator so that it is uniform in depth and coverage.

The second layer of burlap is then added and attached with skewers, pulled taut, and then tacked or stapled in place. The upholsterer now creates the seat's edges and

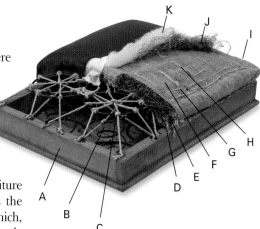

◄ A sample seat showing traditional upholstery structure. Frame (A), webbing (B) affixed to the bottom of it, springs (C) affixed to the frame, burlap (D), first filling (E), second burlap (F), sewing (G), ties (H), perimeter piping (I), second filling (J), cotton batting (K).

▼ View of the seat from the other side. In addition to the previous items, the following can be seen here: muslin (A), leather covering (B), and tacks (C).

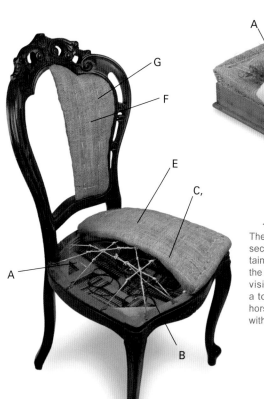

◄ Sample chair showing traditional upholstery. The seat consists of: webbing (A) affixed to the lower section of the frame, springs (B) tied to the frame (certain diagonal webbing is missing here, to better show the structure), burlap (C), first (horsehair) filling (not visible), top burlap (D) and sewing of the set with a topstitch (E). The back rest consists of: burlap, horsehair filling (not visible), and top burlap (F) sewn with a topstitch (G).

◄ Sample armchair with traditional upholstery, more complex than the previous example. The general structure is similar to the previous examples, however, it features springs in the back and arm rests. Both are covered with the set structure (burlap, horsehair, burlap, sewing, batting). The comfort seat features coil springs and a cushion.

► Armchair during upholstering, with springs in the back rest.

silhouette by using traditional upholstery hand stitching techniques.

More ties are added to hold the second filling in place. That filling is also teased to create comfortable and uniform coverage. The second filling is covered with batting or muslin or both, depending on the type of upholstery. Finally, the exterior cover is added and attached to the frame, which may be finished with decorative trim or tacks.

Traditional upholstery: ecological components

The craft involves a new dimension today, with contemporary issues related to environmental consciousness.

Sustainability comes up in three distinct ways. First, the repair of furniture returns it to its function; it can be used again once it is reupholstered. Second, most of the materials used are natural and derived from renewable sources. Once they are taken apart they can be recycled, including the wood of the frames, the metal of the springs and tacks, the different fabrics which make up the upholstery, etc.

It might be added here that these used and disassembled materials, such as the springs and horsehair filling, frequently are able to be reused for other upholstery projects. Generally, good-quality springs do not break; they should be checked for their vertical alignment by pressing on them and observing how they return to their original position. If the spring is not centered it is discarded, together with other metal parts, for later recycling. Clean horsehair filling in good condition can also be saved; it is stored in boxes or bags for later use and, since it is a dry natural fiber, it can last indefinitely if adequately cared for.

With respect to modern upholstery where synthetic materials are used, these materials are derived from oil and hence non-renewable. Large amounts of resources (energy, water, etc.) are needed when making them. These materials are usually of low cost and easy to obtain, and they allow for quicker work than traditional materials; nevertheless, they deteriorate with time, which requires their replacement and an entirely new upholstery job. Furthermore, recycling them is more difficult than with traditional upholstery.

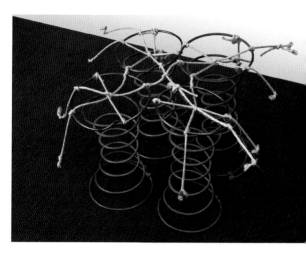

▲ Springs in good condition can be reused for a new upholstery job. The webbing is removed by cutting through the thread tying it to the springs.

◄ Then the cord tying them to the frame is cut, and they are ready to be used once again.

▲ In some cases the filling can also be reused. In this case the seat of the chair had a filling structure in perfect condition, that is, the component made up of the bottom burlap, the interior horsehair, and the top burlap. It was removed and saved for future use. In other cases, it might only be possible to reuse the interior horsehair filling.

▲ A modern furniture seat with latex filling. Latex has a limited lifetime. It deteriorates: it loses its elasticity, falls apart, and turns into powder.

Covering

The exterior covering is the outer layer of the upholstery which is visible once the upholstery has been finished.

Fabrics, leather, or synthetic materials can be used. Selecting the most appropriate one depends on individual creativity, as there is an infinite repertoire of resources, combining shapes, textures, and materials as as well as the various kinds of trims. However, the characteristics of the project, such as the usage of the furniture, should be considered.

A bad choice can result in the exterior covering, tearing or ripping, which would mean the task would have to be done again.

The chosen fabric must be sturdy so it will not rip when it is pulled taut, and it must withstand nailing to the frame of the furniture. Silk fabrics are very delicate, and the holes caused by the tacks or staples are permanent.

Full-grain leather is the best choice when it comes to leather, as it is the most flexible and more supple than other types.

▲ An Art Deco armchair upholstered with silk and linen fabric featuring a geometric pattern.

◄ The choice of each covering fabric depends on personal creativity. Traditional headboards can be upholstered with classic-style fabrics or modern designs, creating attractive contrasts.

► To upholster traditional furniture in classic-style rooms, you can choose a fabric with an updated classic design based on silk.

▼ Furniture can also be uphostered with two or more contrasting fabrics, thereby integrating them into the general decorative style of the room. In this case the upholstery of the modern-style armchairs perfectly matches the furniture and its rustic surroundings. The chosen fabric is a special fireproof material, a good choice for furniture located in front of a fireplace.

In the case of contemporary furniture, you can choose more extreme designs and combine them with smooth and simple fabrics.

One particular type of fabric can be available in different colors. One of the basic factors for choosing the covering is its color.

Fabrics with pictorial elements can be used to decorate contemporary rooms.

Removing the old upholstery	Removing the covering: fabrics, leather, or synthetic materials, decorative trims and tacks Removing the batting, muslin, and upper burlap Examination and saving of the upper horsehair filling if it is in good condition Removing the burlap over the lower filling Examination and saving of the lower filling horsehair if it is in good condition Dismantling the ties of the springs Dismantling the sewing of the springs Examination and saving of the springs if they are in good condition Removing the webbing Removing the tacks or staples from the wooden frame		
Structural work	Basic repairs in the shop, or restoration of the frame by a restorer or specialized carpenter, depending on the type, style, and period of the piece of furniture		
Upholstery work	Seat upholstery	Positioning and affixing of the webbing Positioning and sewing of the springs Tying the springs Placing and sewing of the lower burlap Making the ties for the lower burlap Placing the horsehair for the first filling Placing and sewing of the upper burlap with a top stitch Affixing the upper burlap Affixing and compacting the filling with different stitches (ladder stitch, piping stitch, etc.) Making the ties for the upper burlap Placing the horsehair for the second filling Placing and sewing the batting and/or muslin, depending on the type of upholstery Measuring and preparation (cutting and sewing if necessary) of the covering material Placing and affixing the covering	
	Back rest upholstering	Protecting the covering of the seat with a cloth to avoid staining	
		Simple back	Measuring and preparing the covering material for the rear section of the back rest Placing and affixing the covering of the rear section Placing the batting Placing and affixing the burlap Making the ties Placing the horsehair/filling Applying the batting over the horsehair/filling Measuring and preparation (cutting and sewing if necessary) of the covering material for the front section of the back rest Placing and affixing the front covering
		Back rest without springs	Placing and affixing the webbing Placing and affixing the lower burlap Making the ties Placing the horsehair filling Placing and sewing the upper burlap In certain cases, making the stitch for the furrow In some cases, making the lower back support Placing and affixing the upper burlap In certain cases, affixing and compacting the filling with various stitches (ladder stitch, piping stitch, etc.) Placing and fixation of the batting and/or the muslin, depending on the type of upholstery Measuring and preparation (cutting and sewing if necessary) of the covering material Placing and affixing the covering
		Back rest with springs	The processes are similar to those of the seat
	Upholstering the arm rests	Arm rests without springs	Measuring and affixing of the webbing Placing and affixing the lower burlap Making the ties for the lower burlap Placing the horsehair filling Measuring and sewing of the upper burlap Placing and affixing the upper burlap In certain cases, affixing and compacting the filling using various stitches (ladder stitch, piping stitch, etc.) Making the ties for the upper burlap Placing the horsehair for the second filling Placing and affixing of the batting and/or the muslin depending on the type of upholstery Measuring and preparation (cutting and sewing if required) of the covering material Placing and affixing the covering
		Arm rests with springs	The processes are similar to those of the seat
	Finishing	Fixating the decorative trims (braids, ribbons, tassels, fringes, etc.), piping, and decorative tacks	

These are general processes and they vary depending on the type of the furniture as well as the type of frame and seat.

Basic Techniques

This section explains the basic technical processes to do any kind of traditional upholstery, presented in the general order of the tasks, so it may also provide a general guide to project planning—although the processes must always be adapted to the specific requirements of each case. The modern upholstering system with synthetic materials is included in the section "Cushions" (see page 74) and the first project in the "Step by Step" section (page 89).

◀ Contemporary chair inspired by Louis XV. Painted wood and traditional upholstery with chenille fabric. Tapicería Pons, 2011.

Disassembling the upholstery

One of the most common jobs is the reupholstering of furniture. So it is essential to know the correct methods for disassembling the old upholstery. It must be pointed out that this technique is also used in other processes, such as when extracting tacks after one of the fabric layers of the upholstery has been affixed.

The upholstery is disassembled by removing the various layers that compose it: first the covering, then the filling, the springs, and the webbing. The tacks and staples are removed using the tack puller, paying special attention to avoid marring

◀ **1.** Tacks and fasteners are removed with a tack puller. Here the bottom section of a chair's seat is shown. The tip of the tool is placed parallel to the seat; placing the flat head onto the wood surface with the tool at a slight angle, the head of the tack is held between the two tips and a mallet is used to hammer onto the grip of the tool.

▲ **2.** This results in slighty loosening the tack, which is then lifted using the tack puller as a lever, and extracted with pliers. If necessary the grip of the tool is hammered again with a mallet to move the tack and to remove it.

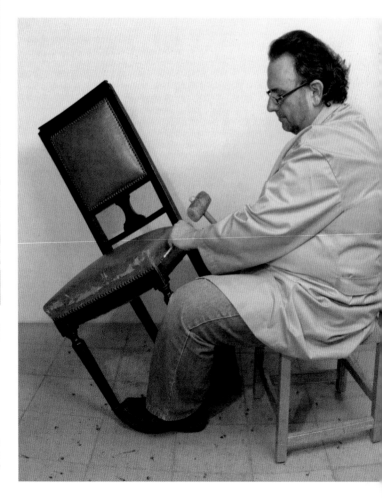

▶ **3.** Generally the most practical method to remove the old upholstery is on a work bench, but in the case of chairs it is done on the floor while seated on another chair. The chair is held between the legs and the tacks holding on the covering, in this case imitation leather, are extracted.

the wood. The cord and thread ties are cut with scissors. The frame must be completely cleaned of all the old elements including staples, tacks, and any other metal pieces before starting the upholstery job.

◀ **4.** The tacks are always removed from the back toward the front to avoid damage to the transom of the back rest; work in sequence, and place the tack puller parallel to the seat.

◀ **5.** Once the tacks have been removed, the vinyl/synthetic leather is removed, as well as the tacks which hold the burlap in place.

TO AVOID

◀ You should never set the tack puller vertically to extract the tacks; that will gouge the wood and leave marks.

▲ **6.** In this case the top set of burlap and filling is in good condition and will be recovered. The ties and the seam are cut with scissors to remove them. Then the process described earlier concerning the remaining upholstery layers is performed.

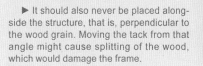

▶ It should also never be placed alongside the structure, that is, perpendicular to the wood grain. Moving the tack from that angle might cause splitting of the wood, which would damage the frame.

Positioning the webbing

The webbing constitutes the base of the upholstery, upon which the other elements and layers for the later processes are placed, so it can be considered to be the foundation. It is essential to position and attach it adequately. It is affixed to the frame while stretching by nailing it from the rear side to the front side of the frame (in the case of the seats) and from the bottom up for the back and arm rests. It is affixed by starting from the central part of the frame and progressing toward the sides; it is helpful to measure and mark the center of the frame edge, including a line to serve as a guide for affixing the webbing. The placing of the webbing must be planned beforehand, and it should be laid out so that once the straps are interlaced no extra space remains. Use the webbing directly from the roll, without cutting, and using the two ends at the same time to avoid wasting material during each webbing installation.

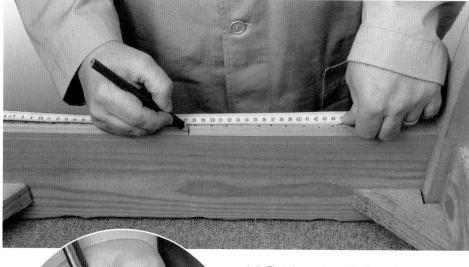

▲ **1.** First the center of the frame is measured and marked.

◄ **2.** A perimeter line at the center of all sides is marked as well, and will act as a guide for affixing the ends of the webbing.

▼ **3.** First the webbing is affixed to the rear section of the frame with its upper end folded inwards, right along the inside of the perimeter pencil mark. This allows it to be aligned perfectly and to be of equal length across, to assure a good final result. It is stapled starting from the center mark.

◄ Before starting work, plan the layout of the webbing, both vertical and horizontal. It is very helpful to try it out beforehand by laying it in place.

◄ **4.** Then the webbing is stretched using the web stretcher; the webbing is passed over the rear part of it and tensioned by pressing its lower section against the frame while the previously rolled-up webbing is held in place as shown (index finger). This method assures an optimal tensioning.

▲ **5.** Then the webbing is stapled to the center and perimeter line as a reference. Once it is stapled it is folded toward the inside and folded once again.

▲ **6.** The stapled webbing. You can observe that it has been distributed evenly with the ends lined up and with equal tension.

◀ **7.** The same process is applied to the transverse webbing, alternatingly interlacing it with the first layer.

▼ **8.** The finished webbing.

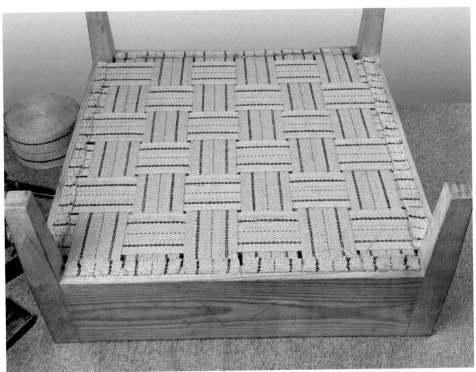

▼ To tension a short length of webbing, for example when the roll is near its end or when it has been cut previously and you want to take advantage of all the material, it is helpful to use pliers.

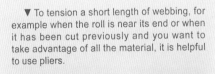

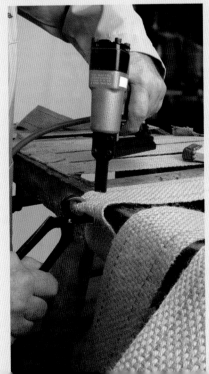

▲ **1.** Before starting out it is essential to distribute and place the springs correctly.

▶ **2.** The springs are placed where they need to be and are affixed to the webbing with thread.

Sewing the springs

Once the webbing is affixed, the springs are placed and attached to the sections that require them. The process is similar in all cases. Sewing keeps the springs fixed to the webbing at the desired position.

Before starting, the placement of the springs is planned, keeping in mind the type of furniture, the area where they will be placed, and its overall size. They are sewn by attaching the lower section of each spring with three ties which should be equidistant. They can also be sewn with four stitches, but three are sufficient to keep them well attached.

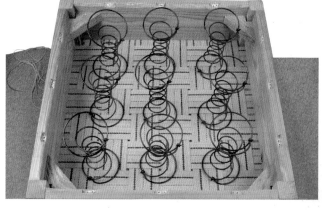

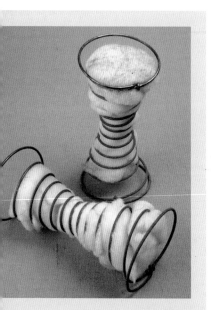

▲ The inside of the springs should not be filled with batting or other material. To obtain their previous, proper tension, springs must be replaced with new ones.

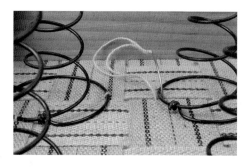

▲ **3.** The springs are sewn to the webbing using the semicircular upholsterer's needle. Start at one end and proceed along one of the lines of springs. The first stitch is performed from below the first ring of the spring, affixed with a sliding knot to tie the thread, and then stitched again downwards. The remaining springs are stitched with three stitches each.

▶ **4.** View of the lower section of the frame with the stitched springs. A final securing knot is made.

Tying the springs

Once the springs have been affixed to the base of the webbing, they are tied with cord at their upper section. This allows for the correct stabilization to maintain the springs in their position so the entire unit can absorb the weight correctly. This process, which is similar for the various applications (seats and rests), is what largely determines the comfort of the upholstery, and impacts the remaining processes. Therefore it is important to work with great precision, paying special attention to the placement and the height of the springs and their correct attachment.

The process is always done in a certain order: first the lengthwise, or front to back, ties are made, then the transverse, or side to side, ties, followed by two diagonal ties; the result is a complex square- and star-shaped web. It is important to make sure that the springs are straight and well-aligned; to adjust their height they are pressed down, to achieve a somewhat higher area in the center when compared to the sides, in the case of seats. The springs should be measured to make sure their height is correct.

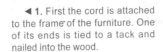

◄ **1.** First the cord is attached to the frame of the furniture. One of its ends is tied to a tack and nailed into the wood.

► **2.** Pass the cord around the top ring of the spring at its center.

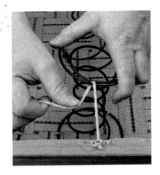

◄ **3.** Turn the cord downwards and pull it up at the top section again, while pressing the spring to position it at its desired height.

► **4.** The process is repeated for the springs in this same line, making sure the cord is centered exactly at each top spring ring. The springs must be at equal distance to each other.

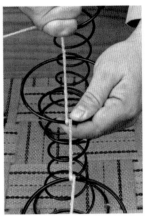

► **5.** To affix the first ties of this section, the cord is passed through two previously-positioned tacks which are only partially nailed into the wood. The cord is placed around the first tack and the cord is pulled taut while pressing down on the spring to position it at the correct height.

▲ **6.** Now the cord is tied around the second tack and secured with a knot. Both tacks are then fully nailed into the wood.

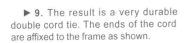

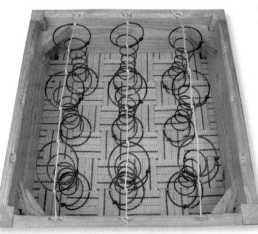

◄ **7.** The completed first lines of tying the springs.

► **8.** The next step is to do the second round of tying, starting again with the first spring, this time in the other direction. In this round, a double knot is used to tie the springs.

► **9.** The result is a very durable double cord tie. The ends of the cord are affixed to the frame as shown.

► **10.** The springs are next tied horizontally, or crosswise. The cord is affixed to the frame, and the springs are tied with double knots. Observe that the horizontal cord passes over the cord of the first round of tying.

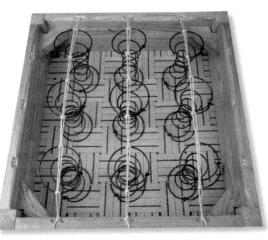

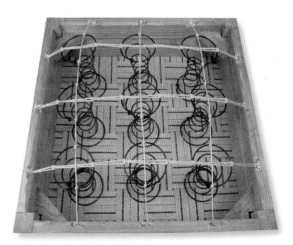

The end of the cord is passed with one hand over the top ring of the spring, while the other hand presses down on it to position it at the correct height. Run the cord under the ring of the spring and return to the other section of the cord passing over it.

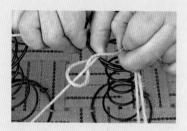

Turn the cord and pass below it, coming out through the central section of the loop.

Secure it by pulling firmly.

Simple or double knots can be used for the ties. This depends on personal preferences, however, double knots are more reliable and are used most often. The following example shows the use of both of them. The double knot is used for the horizontal ties and the simple knot for the diagonal ties. But again, either type of knot may be used.

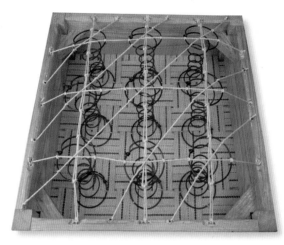

▲ **11.** Now the diagonal ties are made. You can use double knots, although simple knots are shown here. First a diagonal line is tied following the previous process; this time the cord is run over the previous cords at the intersections at the center of the springs.

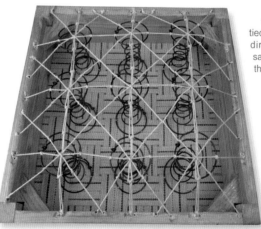

◄ **12.** Then they are tied in the other diagonal direction following the same process. A view of the tied springs.

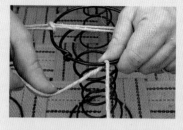

Use one hand to pass the cord through the top ring of the spring and run it downward toward the front, while the other hand presses down on the spring.

The end is run over the previous cord while holding it with the other hand to avoid it slipping from its position.

Then the end is run around the top ring of the spring again toward the inside.

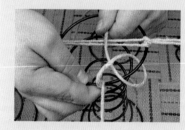

The end is run toward the back.

Pull firmly to secure the cord.

During the entire process, the springs are pressed downward to place them at their correct height. The springs along the edge should be slightly lower than those at the center to make sure the upholstery will be comfortable, since when a person is sitting down on the seat the springs will be at the same height and the weight will be distributed evenly.

▲ **13.** The last diagonal tie is knotted at the intersections of the previous cords, that is, at the center section of the springs and the intersection of the diagonal cords.

Sewing the burlap and the ties

The springs are covered with burlap, which serves as a base for the filling. Again, this process is similar for all parts of the furniture. The burlap is affixed by sewing it to the upper section of the springs, that is, the last rung of the spring. This work is done in a certain order following the arrangement of the springs: each one of them is tied with three stitches. Upholstery thread and needle is used for making a sliding knot at the beginning and another one at the end to finish the task. Once the sewing has been completed the burlap is affixed to the frame along its perimeter. Next, ties are stitched on the burlap to hold the burlap in place and support the filling. They are made by sewing (basting) long stitches to the burlap. The stitches are superimposed on top of each other and have to be sufficiently wide to contain the horsehair/filling.

▲ 1. The burlap piece is cut slightly larger than the area it will cover.

◄ 2. It is positioned over the springs, perfectly centered over the frame of the furniture, and is stitched to the springs using thread and a curved needle. The burlap is affixed to the top spring rung with three stitches. For each spring the needle is passed under the thread just stitched, as shown.

▼ 3. Then it is affixed to the frame and the extra fabric is cut off.

◄ 4. These ties are made using the curved needle and thread. Make long baste-like stitches in the horizontal direction of the frame. The stitch is done by running the needle under the burlap that protrudes at the front. Then return backwards and run the thread under the first stitch.

Filling

To make the filling, horsehair or other material is placed on the burlap and affixed under the ties. The first filling layer is meant to provide shape and comfort to the seat, back, or arm rest. The second filling layer is done the same way: a handful of filling is placed under each tie; then the strands are teased together or worked together to achieve a smooth and uniform layer of the intended thickness.

▶ Sofa made from mahogany and with contemporary silk upholstery, Catalonia, probably Barcelona, made between 1843 and 1868, Ramon Manent collection (photo by Ramon Manent).

◀ **1.** Take a handful of filling, enough to place under a tie, and loosen it by combing so it does not remain compressed and compact; this results in a fluffy filling.

◀▲ **2.** A handful is tucked under a tie, from the rear toward the viewer.

▲ **3.** Then it is rolled around the thread until it has a round shape.

▶ **4.** The strands are separated and distributed for an even surface.

▶ **5.** View of the finished filling.

Sewing

Once the filling is done it is covered again with burlap and then sewn, which provides a firm hold and provides bulk and consistency. Other stitches can be used to shape the edge filling at different areas of the furniture and thus defining the contour of the upholstery.

TOP STITCH

A double-pointed needle is used to perform this stitch. It consists of fixing the layers made up by the filling and the upper burlap to the lower burlap, with a simple stitch; in certain cases the stitch passes below the upper section of the upholstery springs. It is sewn in a straight line, horizontal to the seat, back, or arm rest, making stitches some 3 to 4 inches (8 to 10 cm) apart and separated by ¾ to 1 inch (2 to 3 cm) to cover the entire element. The result: a perfectly assembled set.

▶ Folding screen with walnut frame. The upholstery is traditional-style with a Brussels tapestry covering finished with brass tacks. England, 19th century. A posterior upholstery can be seen here.

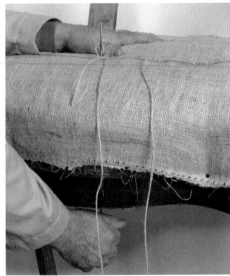

▶ 1. The burlap is placed onto the filling and affixed to the frame with tacks. Then the sewing is done with a top stitch. To make sewing easier, first mark the positions with tailor's chalk. Sewing is done from the back to the front with an initial sliding knot at the end of the stitch in order to secure it. The tip of the needle is passed through the filling until the other end (with the thread) has passed below the bottom burlap.

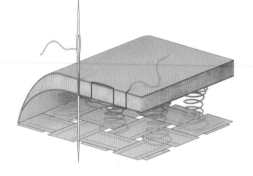
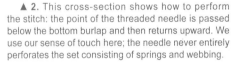

▲ 2. This cross-section shows how to perform the stitch: the point of the threaded needle is passed below the bottom burlap and then returns upward. We use our sense of touch here; the needle never entirely perforates the set consisting of springs and webbing.

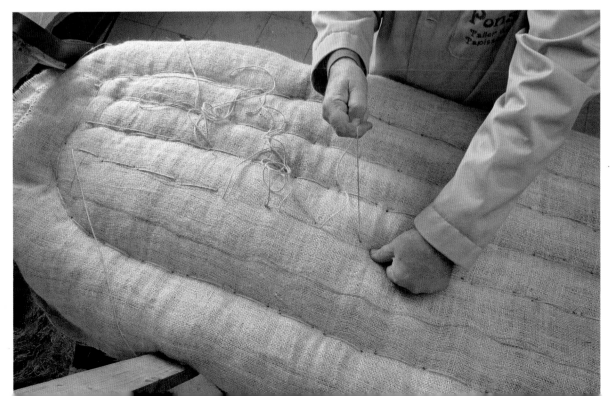

◀ 3. Once each stitch has been made, pull the thread firmly until you get a sturdy and consistent tension (see page 124).

LADDER STITCH

As the name indicates, this stitch is performed by creating parallel stitches which look like the rungs of a ladder. It is used to shape and secure the edge or contour. This stitch is similar to the top stitch, and the stitches are done first from the outside to the inside and then returning to the front; finally, pull the thread taut to fasten the assembly firmly.

For tasks which require the handling of cords and threads by pulling them, it is recommended to use protective gloves (such as biking gloves). You can also make a hand protector from a scrap piece of leather by cutting it to size and making two holes for the thumb.

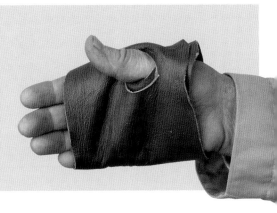

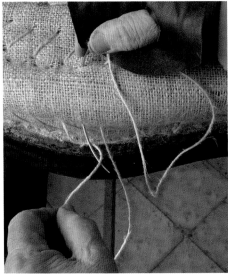

◄ ◄ **1.** The first step consists of threading the upholstering needle from the front toward the back, from the bottom to the top, so that the stitch runs below the desired amount of filling. The needle is taken out from the top section of the stitch.

◄ **2.** Then the forward stitch is done by also running the needle under the filling and the thread of the first stitch, that is, first over and then under it. Then pull firmly to secure the assembly.

BLIND STITCH AND PIPING STITCH

The blind stitch is used to provide consistency to the filling and to fasten it toward the front. The piping stitch is helpful to shape the filling and to create rounded edges, particularly at the arm and back rest. It is done with the same approach used for the previously decribed stitches, making the first stitch from the front toward the inside, and the second stitch where the opposite stitch is located. You need to make sure that the filling is positioned correctly during the entire sewing process by using the regulator tool.

◄ **1.** The blind stitch is done by passing the needle from the front toward the rear, running through part of the filling, and then exiting. Next, as can be seen in the image, the needle is inserted into the same hole, passing it toward the front and exiting at a distance of ¾ inch (2 cm) from the previous one (the distance varies depending on the task). The stitch stays inside the filling and is therefore invisible from the outside.

▶ **2.** Proceed with the piping stitch, by running the upholstery needle from the front toward the back through the filling up to the point where you want the piping to form an edge.

▶ **3.** The needle exits from the top section, and a normal horizontal stitch toward the rear is performed by running the needle between the thread of the previous stitch to tie it, as is done with the ladder stitch. Firmly pull the thread. View of a half-finished arm rest with piping.

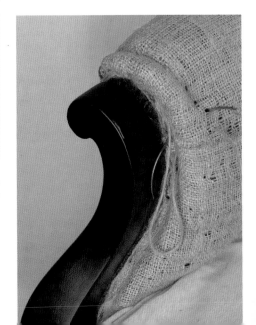

*D*eep buttoning or diamond tufting is the most important technique used for upholstery; however, it is also one of the most difficult ones and requires a lot of practice. It can be applied using the traditional or the modern method (with synthetic materials). In both cases the process is laborious and complex, so for beginners the second method is more accessible.

Traditional tufting requires adequate knowledge concerning ties, filling, sewing, and more. With a little practice you can learn the techniques, though. This section shows the steps involved and explains two different techniques for using muslin as covering: machine sewing, and folding and stitching by hand. Modern tufting is explained step by step (see page 136).

◀ Cromwell sofa consisting of wooden frame and full-grain leather upholstery covering affixed with bronze tacks. Chesterfields, Fleming & Howland, 2011.

◀ **1.** A sample wooden frame of 23½ x 27½ inches (60 x 70 cm) has been built in order to explain the technique, with burlap and a manufactured piping. Given the size of the sample, we have opted for 4$\frac{7}{10}$ x 3$\frac{2}{5}$ inches (12 x 8.75 cm) diamonds so that the side measuring 23½ inches (60 cm) will fit 5 diamonds and the other side of 27½ inches (70 cm) will fit 8 diamonds. Measure and mark the center of the sample on the burlap, mark the width and height of the diamonds at all sides, and then connect them; this will result in the lines which form a grid of squares. Finally, mark the diagonals to obtain the shape of the diamonds (see page 139).

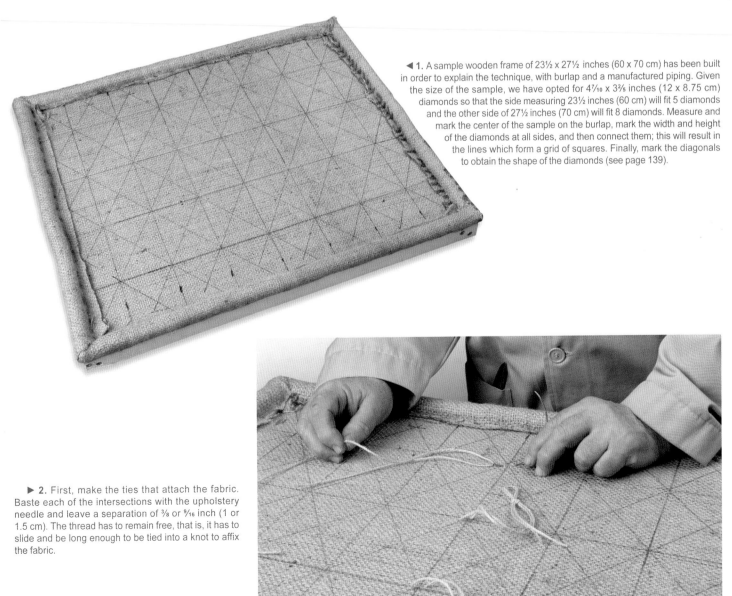

▶ **2.** First, make the ties that attach the fabric. Baste each of the intersections with the upholstery needle and leave a separation of ⅜ or ⁹⁄₁₆ inch (1 or 1.5 cm). The thread has to remain free, that is, it has to slide and be long enough to be tied into a knot to affix the fabric.

▶ **3.** The end of each basting stitch is knotted to prevent the thread from slipping. View of the finished basting of the intersections.

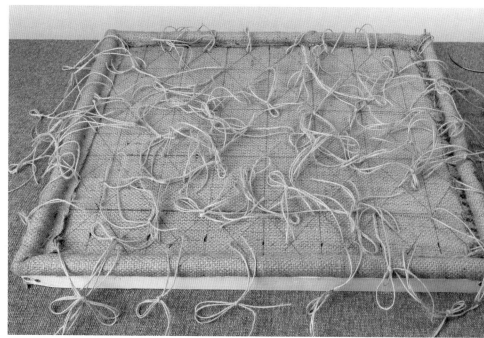

▼ **4.** Then the support ties for the filling are done (see page 58); they are of the same size as the diamonds marked on the burlap. If you don't have much experience you may find it easier to first make the ties and then do the basting at the intersections. Proceed to make the filling, affixing a small ball of filling of similar size to each tie; the bastes will be placed over it.

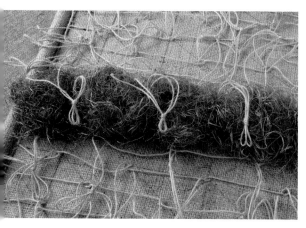

▶ **5.** Once the filling has been finished it is covered with muslin which in this case is sewn with a sewing machine. The location of the diamonds is marked on the back side with tailor's chalk following the previously described process. These diamonds will measure ⁹⁄₁₆ inch (1.5 cm) more at each of their sides compared to the previous diamonds, that is, 1³⁄₁₆ inches (3 cm) longer and wider. The latter measure corresponds to the increase of ⁹⁄₁₆ inch (1.5 cm) of each side of the diamond.

▶ **6.** Stitch with a sewing machine following the pencil marks. The fabric is folded along the center diagonal and sewn, then the rest of the diagonals parallel to it, and finally the other diagonals.

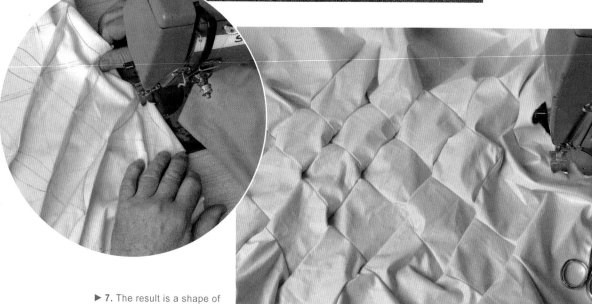

▶ **7.** The result is a shape of diamonds on the muslin.

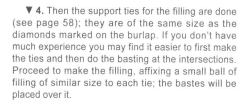

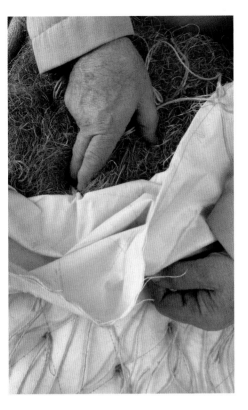

◄ **8.** The muslin is placed centered on the piece (see page 145) and affixed. First the filling is slightly separated by hand in the area of basting to allow for good insertion of the muslin.

▶ **9.** Then the fabric is sewn. The top knot of the basting is loosened and threaded to the upholstering needle, running it through the muslin in the area of one of the points of the diamond, that is, the intersection of diagonals.

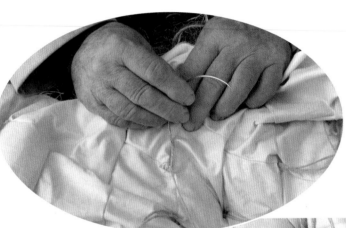

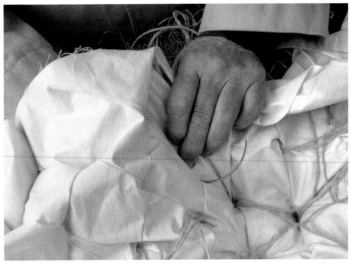

▲ **10.** The thread passes to the top of the muslin. Proceed just as you did with the other end of the thread.

▲ **11.** The other end of the thread should remain separated about ⁹⁄₁₆ inch (1.5 cm) from the first one. Make a knot (see page 64).

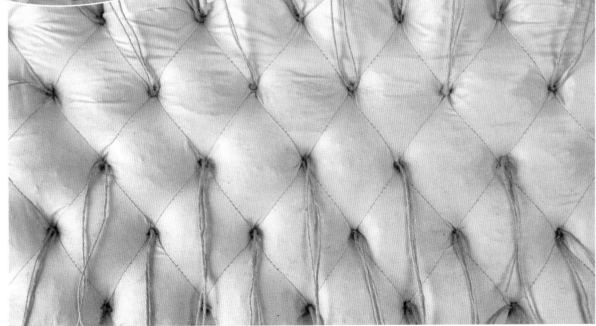

▶ **12.** View of the muslin once it has been placed and affixed.

FOLDED AND HAND-SEWN MUSLIN

▼ **1.** This explains the folding and hand sewing process for the muslin. First mark the muslin as explained in step 17 for the folding, and proceed just as with the machine-sewn stitch, passing both parts of the basting thread at the intersection area, separated about ⁹⁄₁₆ inch (1.5 cm).

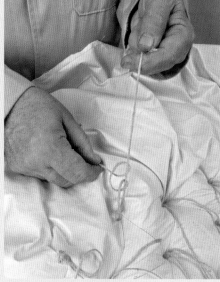
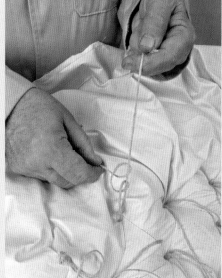

◀ **2.** The muslin is affixed to the filling with a sliding double knot. This step is similar to the machine-sewn process.

▼ **3.** The knot is secured by firmly pulling on the end of thread which has not been knotted, while applying pressure to the knot using the other hand, until it is firm.

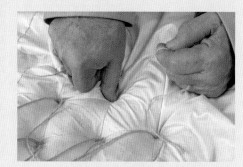

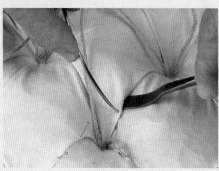

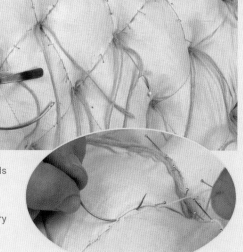

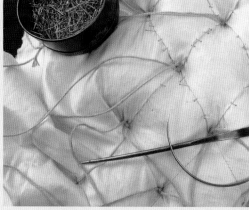

▲ **4.** The muslin (not yet sewn), once it is knotted, looks irregular with many creases. We now make the folds by hand using the regulator tool to position the fabric. The folds are made downward, depending on the furniture or the section that is being worked on. That means folding the fabric at its lower section for a back rest, and at the front for a seat.

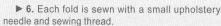

▲ **5.** View of the hand-folded muslin. The folds are provisionally affixed with pins.

▶ **6.** Each fold is sewn with a small upholstery needle and sewing thread.

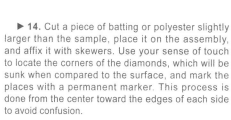

◀ **13.** The double-pointed needle is used to pass one of the thread ends to the rear of the assembly, so that only one end of the thread remains at the front.

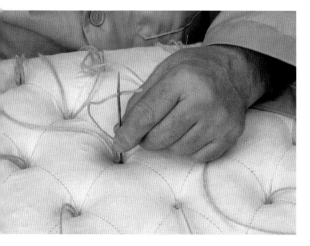

▶ **14.** Cut a piece of batting or polyester slightly larger than the sample, place it on the assembly, and affix it with skewers. Use your sense of touch to locate the corners of the diamonds, which will be sunk when compared to the surface, and mark the places with a permanent marker. This process is done from the center toward the edges of each side to avoid confusion.

◄ 15. The filling is removed and perforated with a punch iron. Place it on a piece of wood to avoid damaging the surface below. Position the punch perfectly vertical on the mark and hammer firmly to cut out the holes.

▼ 16. Use scissors to make a cross cut to open the holes; this cut facilitates the placement of the threads and their attachment. Then the filling is placed onto the set and the threads are passed through the holes. Finally it is stapled to the frame.

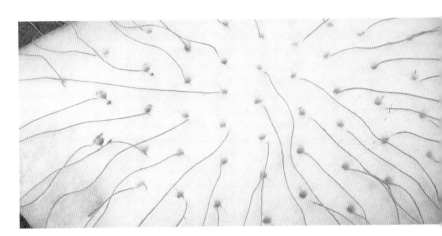

► 17. Following the process described earlier, the placement of the diamonds is marked on the covering fabric with tailor's chalk (see page 62).

▼ 18. The fabric is placed centered onto the assembly so that the intersection of the diagonals matches to the threads (see page 63). It is affixed starting from the center and progressing toward the edges. Thread the upholstery needle with the tufting twine and run it through the wrong side of the fabric, positioning it next to the intersection of the diagonals, almost ⅜ inch (1 cm) on both sides of that intersection.

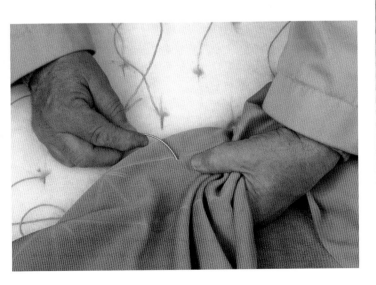

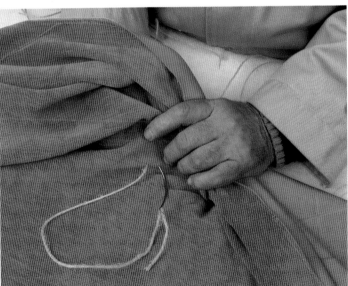

▲ 19. The needle is pulled out from the top side of the fabric and reinserted 9/16 to ¾ inch (1.5 to 2 cm) away from the previous stitch.

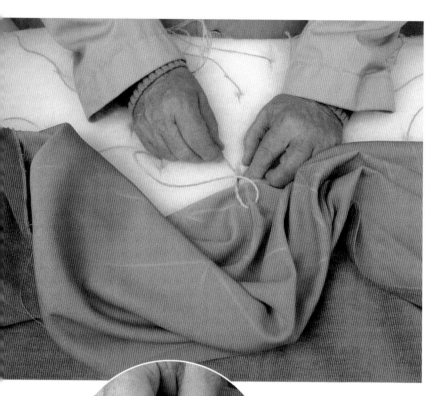

◄ 20. Finally the thread is run through the hole in the filling and to the other side of the burlap which makes up the base of this sample. After it is run through, it is knotted at the back with the first end of the basting (see step 13).

▼ 21. The folds of the fabric are made with the regulator tool and a skewer and placed as desired. The folds are always made downwards, in line with the direction of the upholstered element, in this case the direction of the fabric—that is, with the velvet nap facing downwards as well, never against the nap.

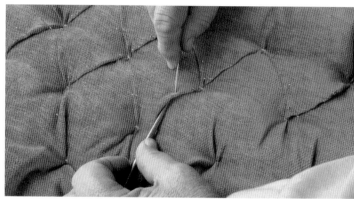

◄ 22. Hold the folds in place with pins while making them.

► 23. Work in order, affixing the assembly with pins.

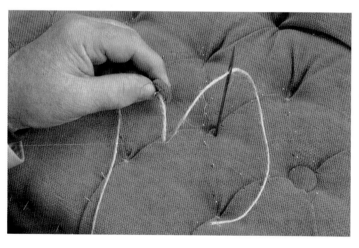

▲ 24. Once the buttons have been made (see the following section), they are sewn to the assembly with twine and a double-pointed needle. The button is threaded onto one of the thread ends, and the needle is inserted at almost ⅜ inch (1 cm) from the previous stitch, passing through the back side of the burlap.

► 25. The finished sample.

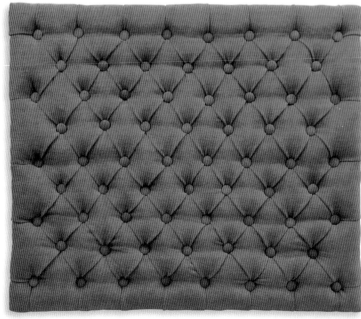

Making buttons

The manufacturing of any tufted upholstery requires making buttons, which must be covered with the material used for the rest of the work or with contrasting material. They are easy to make if you have a button machine available. In this case the buttons are covered with full-grain cow leather, but the process is similar for other coverings such as fabrics.

▲ **2.** The punch iron allows for making multiple cuts at the same time, quickly and precisely; in this case four pieces are obtained. In addition, a cardboard template can be made to facilitate the cutting of the material. The size depends on the interior size of the upper die; for example, size 18 buttons, a common size, are $7/16$ inch (1.1 cm) in diameter.

▶ **1.** The covering is cut based on the size of the buttons and the machine mold. The leather is placed onto a thick wooden support (to avoid leaving marks) and folded over in order to cut several pieces at once. Make the cut by hammering on the perfectly vertical punch iron.

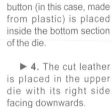

◀ **3.** The base of the button (in this case, made from plastic) is placed inside the bottom section of the die.

▶ **4.** The cut leather is placed in the upper die with its right side facing downwards.

▶ **5.** Then the top piece of the button is inserted into the set at the interior of the mold with the wooden tip.

▶ **6.** Both pieces are placed into the machine.

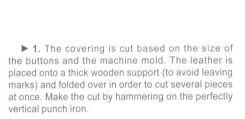

▼ **7.** Firmly press the lever.

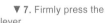

◀ **8.** The result is the insertion of the lower piece of the button into the top piece, holding the covering on the button.

Sewing non-traditional tufted buttons

For modern tufting using modern materials (see page 136), a different method is used for sewing the buttons. The materials are flexible enough to allow for knotting and sewing the buttons with the same thread, which provides the cushioning typical of tufting and allows one to make the folds.

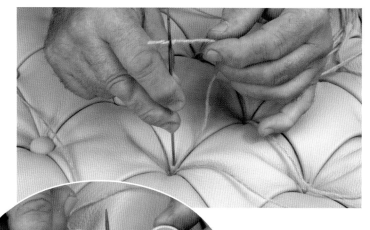

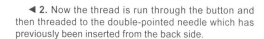

◀ **1.** First one of the thread ends is threaded (the short end) which has been previously knotted (see page 148) to the double-pointed needle and then stitched so it comes out at the back end. The result is that only the long end of the thread is on the upholstered side.

◀ **2.** Now the thread is run through the button and then threaded to the double-pointed needle which has previously been inserted from the back side.

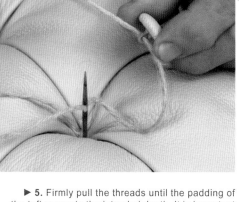

◀ **3.** The button is held with one hand while the needle is pulled with the other hand.

▶ **4.** The needle must be separated some ⁹⁄₁₆ inch (1.5 cm) from the exit point of the thread. Pass it toward the back side of the upholstery while the end of the thread also stays there (see page 148).

▶ **5.** Firmly pull the threads until the padding of the tuft presents the intended depth. It is important to exercise even force for each one, to achieve a uniform tuft. To control the depth of the buttons on the upholstered side, it helps to have another person assist you.

◀ **6.** The thread is affixed to the rear side with a double knot.

◀ **7.** Finally, stitch the long end of the thread to the webbing using the upholstering needle, and when exiting pass through the interior of the stitch to knot it.

▶ **8.** Cut off the extra thread with scissors.

Calculating the Fabric and Making Elements

*O*ne basic aspect of any upholstery work is to correctly calculate the amount of covering (fabric, leather or synthetic material). This is a very important process since the final look of the work largely depends on it.

The final covering, that is, placing and applying it, also may require the making of special elements in the shop. The creation of these items requires some machine sewing, which is not explained here in detail as it exceeds the limits of this book, but which is within reach for anyone with some practice.

Calculating the covering

The correct calculation of the covering requires accurately measuring the sections of the piece of furniture. While it adjusts a bit for each type of piece, the method is always similar. In most cases the elements which compose the piece of furniture are rectangular, which facilitates the marking and cutting of the covering as well as the upholstery work. Measuring an armchair is the example shown here. Although it is fairly complex, it uses the steps that are needed in most other projects. The measurements are taken in order, according to which pieces of the item are involved in the final upholstery.

MEASURING AN ARMCHAIR

The seat is measured: first the depth and then the width. The measurements must be as precise as possible, so the measuring tape is run below the back rest until it reaches the edge of the rear wooden frame. Do likewise with the width.

The total length of the arm rest is measured. The tape is run from the lower edge of the frame, curving over it up to its lower section. The width is measured from the rear section to the front center.

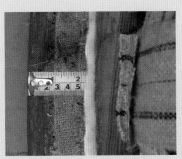

The back rest is measured similarly to the seat (height and width), running the tape under it up to the structure, or from one part of the frame to the other.

The wings are measured the same way: the height from its lower section up to the rear frame, and its width from the outermost part up to the frame.

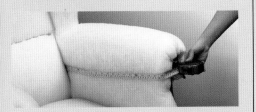

The outside of the arm rest is also measured, both height and width, at the most protruding part of the frame or structure.

The procedure is similar for the outer sides of the wings. Measure from the lower part of the frame up to the highest point of the element, including the maximum width.

Proceed likewise at the rear side of the back rest, taking into account the frame.

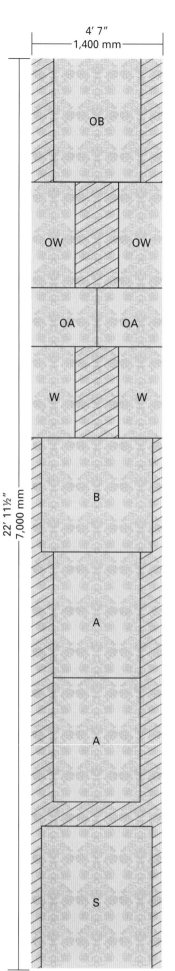

4' 7"
1,400 mm

OB

OW   OW

OA   OA

W   W

B

A

A

S

22' 11½"
7,000 mm

◀ Template of correct planning for a stamped-pattern fabric for the armchair. Seat (S), arms (A), back rest (B), wings (W), outer arms (OA), outer wings (OW), and outer back rest (OB).

Once the measuring is done the measurements are transferred onto the covering, adding about 2 inches (5 cm) to each side, that is, an extra 4 inches (10 cm) for every section. For this armchair, chenille fabric that is about 1½ yards (1.45 m) wide is used, and about 7⅔ yards (7 m) is required.

Sometimes the width of the fabric may not be sufficient to make certain pieces; in such cases it is necessary to make stretchers to affix the fabric (see page 132). When using print fabrics it is essential to plan the layout of the pieces before measuring and marking them. The main motifs of the pattern should be centered on the seat, the back, and the arm rests, and also keep in mind the back sides of the piece of furniture if applicable.

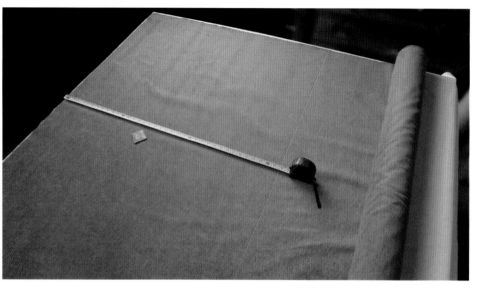

◀ **1.** The first step is to transfer the measurements onto the fabric you are using for the covering, adding 4 inches (10 cm) to each side; these measurements are marked on the wrong side of the fabric using tailor's chalk.

▶ **2.** Whenever chenille fabric is used (this also applies to velvet) it is important to mark the fabric grain. It should point downward, that is, from the top to the bottom and from the back to the front depending on the element. To prevent possible mistakes a chalk line of the section is marked on the back side of the fabric, in this case an arm rest. It is also handy to mark the piece with the number corresponding to the order of work steps (in this case the second, after the seat) and whether it is the left or the right side of the furniture.

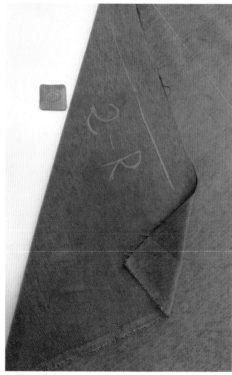

◀ **3.** The photo shows the two sections of chenille that will cover the arms of the armchair. Note the chalk marks to use in correctly placing the fabric.

Making elements

PIPING

In many cases the upholstering requires the creation of piping with a covering similar to the rest of the upholstery. It is quick and easy to make; a manufactured cording is covered with the desired fabric. It is a good practice to always make pieces like this slightly longer than needed to avoid problems and to be able to make changes if required.

SEAMS

It is often necessary to make seams between sections of the covering material for upholstering very wide seats or lateral sections. The process is simple and presents no major problems when you use a sewing machine. It is easy to make seams with piping between the pieces of material.

▲ The piping/cording is made in the shop by covering the cord with the covering, in this case brown full-grain leather, using a sewing machine.

▼ **1.** To make the seam, the cut pieces are perfectly aligned using a straight stitch. In this example, the lateral piece is seamed for a headrest which is upholstered with full-grain leather (see page 150).

▼ **2.** Then the seam is reinforced by sewing a piece of fabric to the back side. In this case it would also be possible to use a scrap piece of leather.

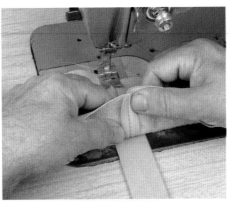

▲ **3.** Make an open backstitch with the sewing machine.

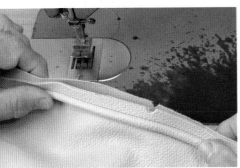

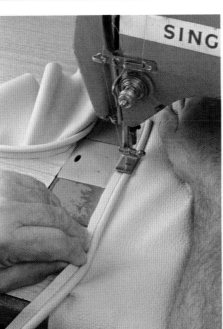

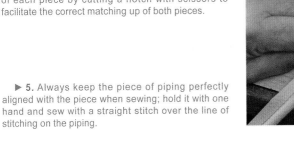

▲ **4.** Before sewing in the piping, mark the center of each piece by cutting a notch with scissors to facilitate the correct matching up of both pieces.

▶ **5.** Always keep the piece of piping perfectly aligned with the piece when sewing; hold it with one hand and sew with a straight stitch over the line of stitching on the piping.

▲ **6.** The result is piping attached with stitching which, once the upholstering is finished, will be invisible.

Other Techniques

A part from the typical traditional processes, there are other special techniques. Repair of upholstered pieces requires techniques that complement the traditional methods. The repairs should always aim to return integrity to the upholstery, and should never be simply a patch. It is more effective to completely reupholster the item, even if that requires more time and expense, than to just patch it, which might in the end mean that before long the piece will require a complete redo anyway. This section explains how to repair a seat from below, the most common repair in upholstery.

A widely used technique today is padding. This technique is simpler and faster than tufting, which it is vaguely similar to, and it does not require advanced knowledge of upholstery; this makes it very accessible to people who want to being doing upholstery. Nevertheless the results from padding can be very interesting and in line with current decor trends.

A commonly-seen example of upholstery damage is the breaking of the underside of the seat, caused by deteriorating webbing from the continuous use of the furniture. Usually a new upholstering job is recommended; however, if the filling and the covering are in good condition, the seat can be fixed at the bottom side. The following explains the method to use. It will also be necessary to change the covering of the chair's seat. Essentially the repair process consists of creating a rigid support structure for the springs and the new webbing.

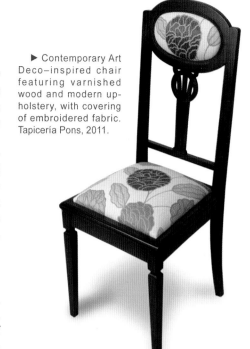

▶ Contemporary Art Deco–inspired chair featuring varnished wood and modern upholstery, with covering of embroidered fabric. Tapicería Pons, 2011.

▲ **1.** The most common damage seen in chairs is broken straps of webbing, which is the foundation of the upholstery.

▶ **2.** First the webbing is removed using the tack puller (see page 50). Then cut the threads that tie it to the springs and remove them.

◀ **3.** The structure that supports the springs is made from thick stainless steel wire. Eight metal fasteners are nailed to the center of the lower part of the frame next to each spring.

◀ **4.** The wire is run through the first fastener at one of the sides, bent, and then firmly hammered to the wood.

◀ **5.** The wire is run to the fastener on the opposite side of the frame and pulled taut with pliers. Place a piece of rubber under the pliers to prevent damage to the wood, and use them as a lever. Hammer the fastener into the wood, cut off the extra wire, and wrap the end with the pliers as shown.

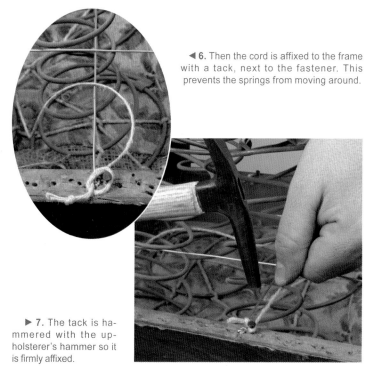

◄ **6.** Then the cord is affixed to the frame with a tack, next to the fastener. This prevents the springs from moving around.

► **7.** The tack is hammered with the upholsterer's hammer so it is firmly affixed.

▲ **8.** Once the structure is done and the cord is affixed to the two sides of the frame, the springs are placed under the wire support. Press down on them and put them into their correct position.

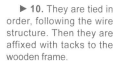

◄ **9.** The springs are tied between them and to the wire frame using double knots to prevent them from slipping. The ties are made parallel to the wire.

► **10.** They are tied in order, following the wire structure. Then they are affixed with tacks to the wooden frame.

▲ **11.** Finally the webbing is affixed to the lower part of the frame following the previously described process (see page 62).

► **12.** The repaired chair.

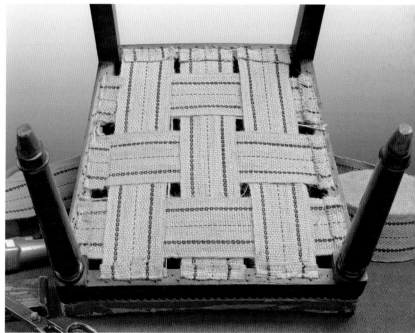

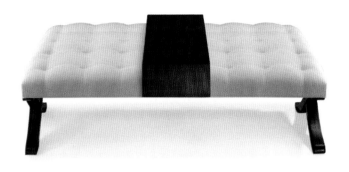

▲ Ottoman coffee table, made of mahogany with upholstered padding of Alcantara, with top pull-out tray. Christopher Guy, 2011.

Padding

Padding consists of creating symmetrically pulled buttons in the upholstery with some sunken sections; a padded grid is created, reminiscent of tufting, although this technique involves different processes. Padding uses synthetic materials and modern techniques, and although it uses basic processes, the result is attractive. The following example shows the method for making a headrest, but the technique can be used for all kinds of elements: seats or back rests as well as furniture not used for seating such as tables, stools, folding screens, etc.

Padding can be made in different shapes and sizes. Essentially it consists of doing the upholstery on a rigid support with openings, which are used to knot the pulled sections of the padding. The final look is very compatible with contemporary decorating styles.

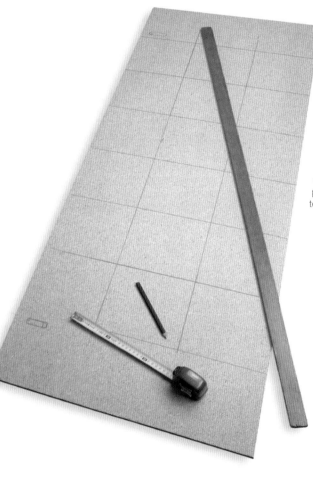

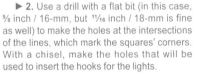

◀ **1.** A ¾-inch-thick (2 cm) sheet of plywood is used to make the headboard of about 23⅝ x 63 inches (60 x 160 cm). The padding is done in squares of 7⅞ x 7⅞ inches (20 x 20 cm). First mark the placement points on the frame, as well as the holes under the plates which are used to affix the headboard to the wall.

▶ **2.** Use a drill with a flat bit (in this case, ⅝ inch / 16-mm, but ¹¹⁄₁₆ inch / 18-mm is fine as well) to make the holes at the intersections of the lines, which mark the squares' corners. With a chisel, make the holes that will be used to insert the hooks for the lights.

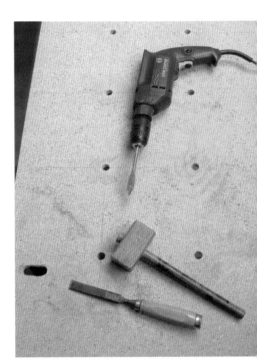

▼ **3.** A 1³⁄₁₆-inch-thick (3 cm) piece of polyurethane foam of density 30 is cut to a similar size as the frame, and stapled to the edge of the board with ¼-high (6 mm) staples. Start stapling from the center out toward both sides. This prevents any uneven sections.

▼ **4.** Then a piece of batting of density 300 is cut, slightly larger than the headboard. It is placed onto the headboard so that there is extra material on all sides, and then temporarily attached with skewers. Then it is attached to the side of the headboard (edge) with the same staples used previously, and the extra material is cut off.

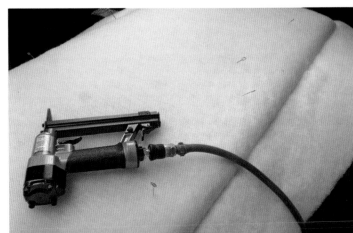

◄ **5.** To mark the placement of the board's holes, use a long double-pointed needle. It is inserted at the back for each hole, and the point where it sticks out from the padding is marked with a permanent marker.

► **6.** Then the padding is cut in the shape of a cross at each mark using scissors, which will help to correctly place the fabric.

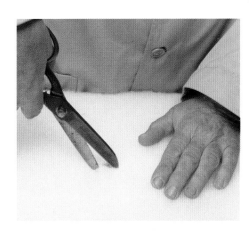

► **7.** In this case vinyl/synthetic leather is used for the covering. In order to affix the stitches to the frame without buttons, it is necessary to sew strips of fabric to the back side of the covering following the placement of the padding. The image shows the seam lines on the right side of the vinyl/synthetic leather.

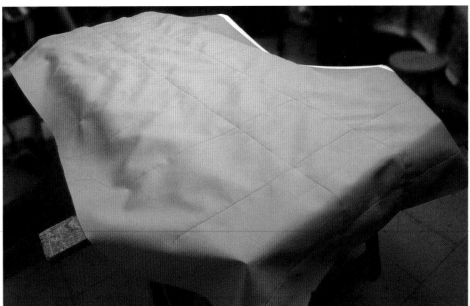

▼ **8.** The placement of the squares, 7⅞ x 7⅞ inches (20 x 20 cm), is measured and marked with a pencil on the back side of the vinyl/synthetic leather. Then the sewing machine is used to sew a strip which has a lengthwise fold by following the lines.

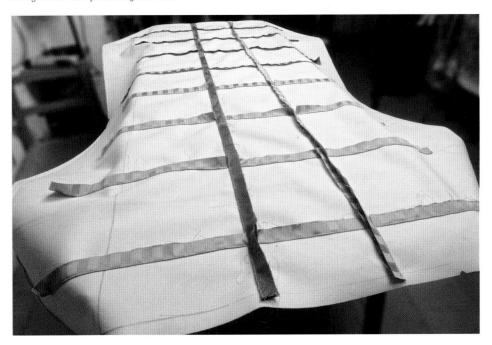

▼ **9.** Note that the vertical bands have been cut at the intersections to allow for the correct sewing of the two horizontal bands.

► **10.** To attach the threads which will hold the padding, stitch them to the intersections of the bands using the upholstery needle. The thread should be long enough to make all of the stitches needed.

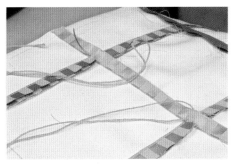

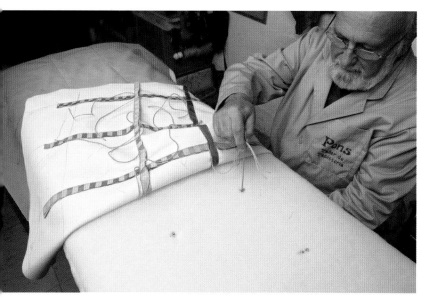

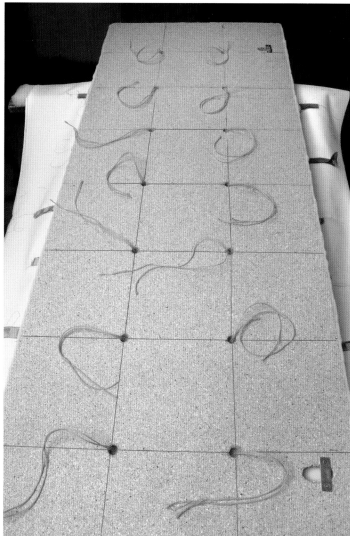

▲ **11.** The vinyl/synthetic leather covering is carefully placed on the headboard so that the threads match the holes cut into the padding. Then the two ends of each thread are passed toward the back of the headboard with the double-pointed needle. The process begins at the center of the board and from there moves toward the sides.

▶ **12.** View of the thread after it is passed toward the back. Note that the plates (2 x ⁹⁄₁₆ inches / 5 x 1.5 cm) have been attached to the rear of the board to mount it to the wall.

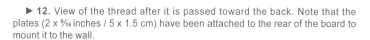

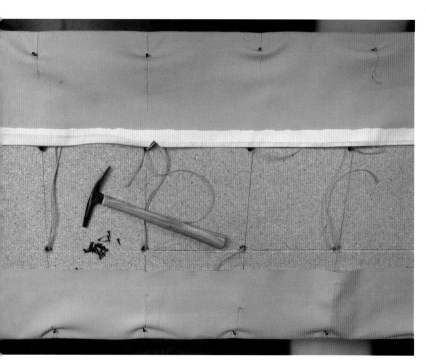

▲ **13.** The vinyl/synthetic leather, pulled taut, is temporarily tacked to the back of the headboard.

▶ **14.** Then it is affixed with staples similar to the ones used for affixing the polyurethane foam and the padding. Start from the center of each side and work toward the edges.

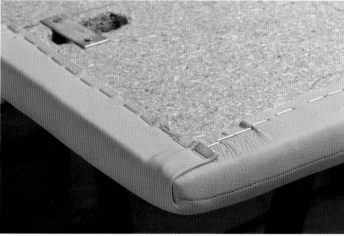

▲ 15. First the vertical sides of the headboard are affixed, then the top and bottom edges, that is, the horizontal sides. To finish the four corners the vinyl/synthetic leather of the horizontal edges is folded over the vertical edges.

► 16. The stitches of the padding are marked at the rear section of the headboard. This process is best done with another person: while one person pulls the threads and attaches them, the other person checks that the recessed sections are at the same depth. It is helpful to make a tool like the one shown, consisting of a wooden strip about a yard (meter) long, with a perpendicular peg marking the desired depth. This brace acts as a level with respect to the surface of the upholstery, while the peg shows the correct depth.

► 17. Staples are used to secure the threads (two for each stitch) to the headboard. First, staple in one direction several times and then repeat the process while alternating between forward and backward. Cut off the extra thread.

▼ 18. Finally, the rear section of the headboard is covered with white fabric attached with staples. Use scissors to make a cut into the fabric where the hook will be inserted into the plate.

▼ 19. View of the finished headboard.

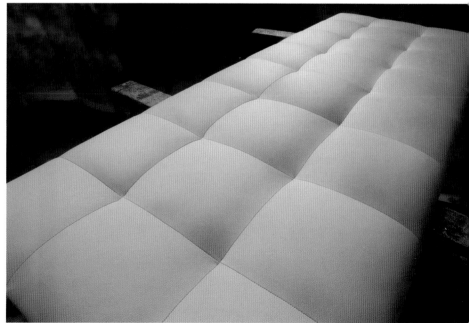

Canework Techniques

▼ Contemporary chair consisting of varnished wood with canework seat and back rest. Tapiceria Pons, 2009.

Canework is traditionally part of basket-making—which also involves the typical processes of upholstery—so it is somewhere in between the two disciplines. It is used to make rests, seats, and other elements of furniture, and is done at upholstery workshops. It consists of a web of plant-fiber bark or stems which are woven and affixed to the frame of a piece of furniture. Depending on the design of each piece, canework can be made from pre-manufactured sections, or woven into the holes of the frame.

Both methods are shown here. The second one includes the cleaning and fitting processes needed to replace broken canework with new canework to restore a piece of furniture.

Machine-woven webbing

This is the most common technique for modern furniture, particularly furniture that undergoes daily use in the work or home environment. It involves fastening premade canework inside the rabbet in the frame of the piece of furniture, and covering that with a length of binder cane.

▶ **1.** First a section of machine-woven webbing is cut, slightly larger than the area which needs to be covered, along with a section of binder cane somewhat longer than the groove outline. They are soaked for about 20 minutes in a large container with sufficient water.

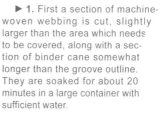

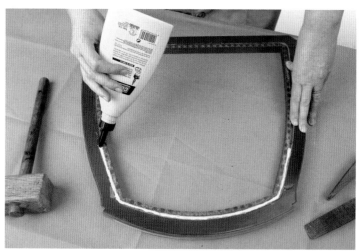

▲ **2.** The frame is placed on the work bench and PVA glue is applied to the inside of the groove. It must be absolutely clean, without any remnants of old glue.

◀ **3.** The cane webbing is removed from the water and placed on the frame, perfectly centered.

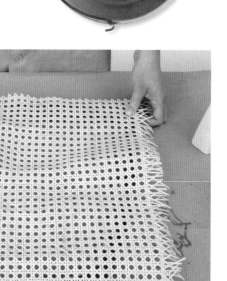

▶ **4.** Then the canework is inserted into the groove using a wedge which is held vertically while hammering it with a wooden mallet. Work from the rear of the seat toward the sides, and from there toward the front. Choose the most appropriate wedge for the width of the groove.

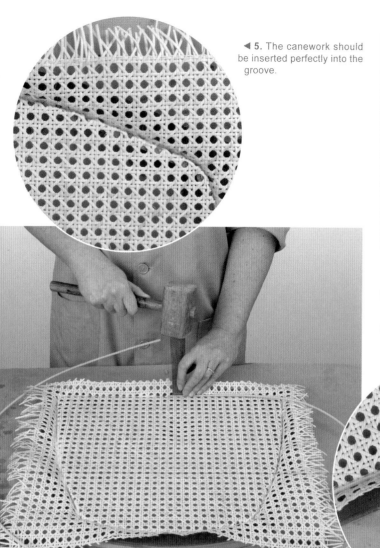

◄ 5. The canework should be inserted perfectly into the groove.

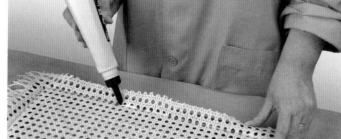

▲ 6. Then the groove is finished, using the binder cane. A PVA glue line is applied along the insertion groove.

◄ 7. Use a wedge with a wide tip to insert the binder cane into the groove. Start at the front of the seat and continue all the way around.

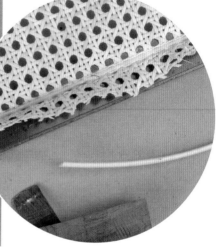

◄ 8. Note that the joining of the cane is done diagonally by cutting both ends at an angle to achieve an almost imperceptible joint.

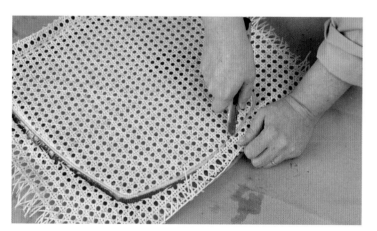

▲ 9. Cut off the extra cane with a very sharp cutter and clean any remnants of glue with a damp cloth before it dries. Then dry the wood with a clean rag.

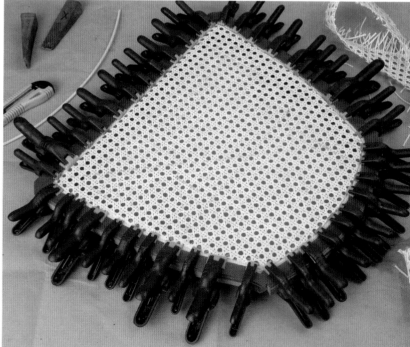

► 10. The seat is secured with clamps placed along the perimeter. Allow at least 24 hours for the glue to dry completely, and remove the clamps.

Woven canework

Caning consists of the square and diagonal weaving of cane strips to create a uniform grid, resulting in a strong and resilient fabric. The canes are threaded through the holes bored into the frame and are then interwoven. This method is used for antique as well as modern furniture; it requires some skill but it is not overly complicated. When this method is used for antique furniture the steps for preparing the frame are very important, including the removal of the old canework and the cleaning of the holes before weaving the new canework. Keep in mind that the canework will vary depending on the shape of the seat or back rest of each piece of furniture; but the method is similar for all shapes.

In most cases the holes of the back rests are blind, meaning they do not go all the way through the frame, so the canes are placed into the holes and glued.

The Isabel-style chair shown here demonstrates the most common current system to do caning, including the processes for removing the existing broken caning and preparing the frame.

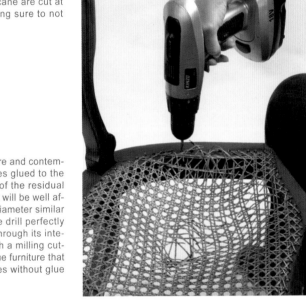

◄ **1.** The first step is to remove the old canework, which has suffered considerable damage due to improper use. To do this the connecting strands of the canework and the perimeter binder cane are cut at the holes using a cutter, while making sure to not mark the wood.

► **2.** Both restored antique furniture and contemporary pieces usually have the canes glued to the frame. It is important to remove all of the residual glue to make sure the new canework will be well affixed. Use a drill with a drill bit of a diameter similar to the holes; the idea is to insert the drill perfectly vertical into each hole and to bore through its interior, or if necessary a rotary tool with a milling cutter of similar size can be used. Antique furniture that has not been restored features canes without glue so this process is not necessary.

◄ **3.** Then the canework for the seat is made. First the layer of dust below the original canework is removed to keep it from staining the new canes which have been placed into water to soak. Mark the center of the seat by placing two tees into the front and rear holes.

◄ **4.** Cane of 2.25 mm is used. The ends of two canes are placed into the rear center hole. Add a drop of white glue and hold it in place to dry by inserting a tee.

▶ **6.** One by one the aligned canes are passed through the holes; proceed from the center toward the sides.

▼ **5.** The two canes are run across the top part of the frame, perfectly aligned, toward the front center hole of the seat; they are pulled taut but not too much as they might break. Then they are run through the hole, from top to the lower part of the frame; they are secured with a tee.

▶ **7.** The ends are secured with strips of glue. They are held in place with a tee whenever required. The canes have to be perfectly aligned and at even distances with respect to the holes of the frame.

In antique furniture it is common to find that the holes are not equidistant. They are skipped when necessary, placing the canes into the holes most appropriate for good alignment.

▶ **8.** Allow the glue to dry for at least 24 hours. The tees are then removed. View of the vertical canes.

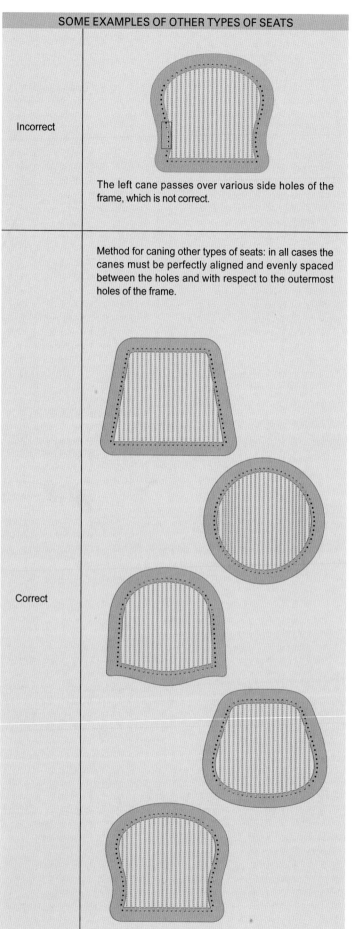

SOME EXAMPLES OF OTHER TYPES OF SEATS

Incorrect

The left cane passes over various side holes of the frame, which is not correct.

Method for caning other types of seats: in all cases the canes must be perfectly aligned and evenly spaced between the holes and with respect to the outermost holes of the frame.

Correct

▲ **9.** Next, the start of weaving the horizontal canes from the front of the seat. The first horizontal cane's approximate placement is marked with two tees, and the two hoops are woven alternatingly.

▲ **10.** The first cane is run through the hoop's eye and passed through. The long hoop without eye stays still and is moved only to help with the weaving. The second cane is passed through the same way, alternating with the first one, and the short hoop is moved depending on the large one's position.

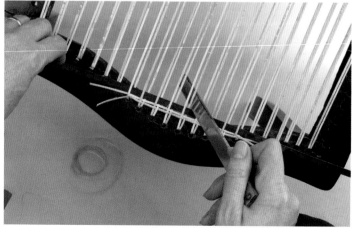

▲ **11.** Then the extra material is cut with cutting pliers and the canes are placed as desired, gently pounding the iron rod on the long cane.

▶ **12.** The ends of the canes are threaded into the holes of the frame, centered, affixed with a drop of glue, and secured with tees.

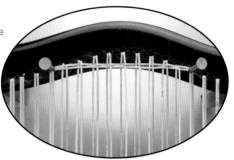

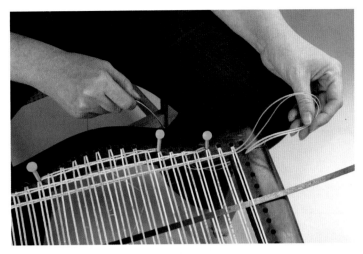

▶ **13.** Proceed in order toward the central part of the seat, making the second horizontal run and affixing it. At the third run the canes are introduced through the first hole of the lateral side; they run below the frame and exit through the following hole.

▶ **14.** The third run is secured with a tee and the next one is made by alternatingly passing through the canes as described. Proceed to weave the canework for as long as the length of each cane allows, and affix and secure the end with glue and a tee.

◀ **15.** The task continues toward the center of the seat, but without getting that far. Then the rear section is done. The caning is done this way because as the weaving progresses the structure becomes more rigid, and it would be difficult to make the short runs at the rear; it is easier to finish the long runs of the center.

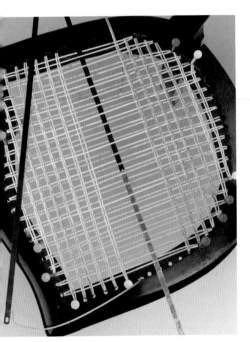

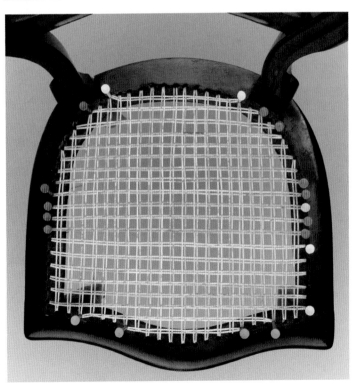

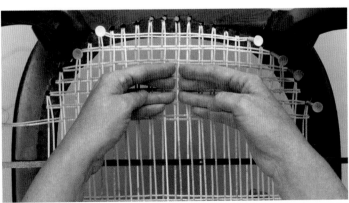

▲ **16.** While the work is progressing, adjust the placement of the canes with yours hands so the grid stays uniform.

▲ **17.** View of the horizontal runs when finished. The glue must dry for 24 hours, then the tees are removed.

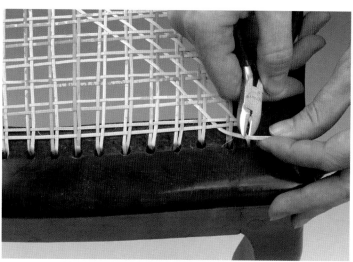

▲ **18.** Now the diagonal run of the canes is done, first along one diagonal and then in the other direction. The first diagonal is performed by running the cane under the vertical run of the seat where its cane passes over the horizontal ones. If the first vertical cane runs under the horizontal ones, then the diagonal will pass over them.

▲ **19.** Once the cane has been set it is cut and introduced into the hole of the frame.

▶ **20.** View of the finished first diagonal.

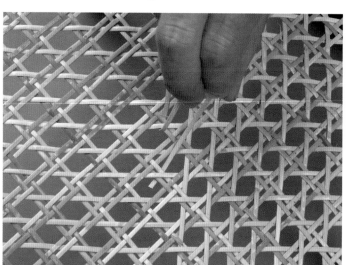

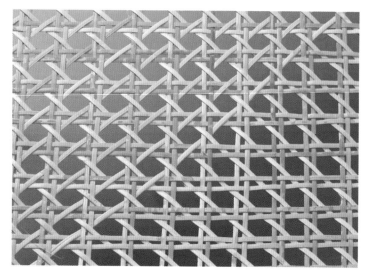

▲ **21.** Proceed likewise with the second diagonal, passing the canes one by one under the horizontal ones and over the vertical runs of the grid.

▲ **22.** View of the second diagonal during the process.

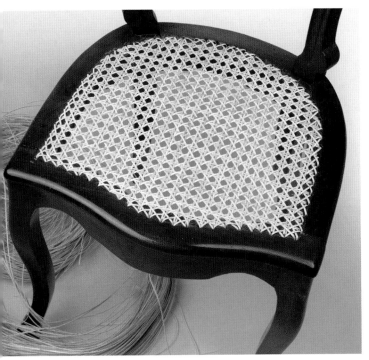

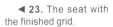
◄ **23.** The seat with the finished grid.

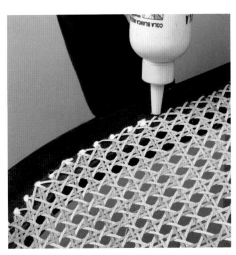

► **24.** Now the perimeter edging of the seat is made. One drop of glue is placed into each hole of the frame, starting at the rear part of the seat and up to its center.

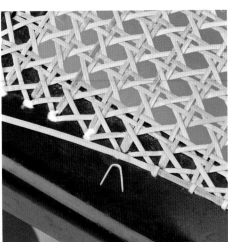

► **25.** A cane is placed onto the line of the holes of the frame with curved sections of anchor pieces. These sections are about one and a half fingers long. They are placed into the holes.

◄ **26.** The cane is positioned into each hole with a screwdriver or similar flat-ended tool. The same is done with the short sections. One side is done first and then the other, uniting both ends of the cane at the front center section of the seat. The glue should dry for 24 hours.

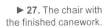
► **27.** The chair with the finished canework.

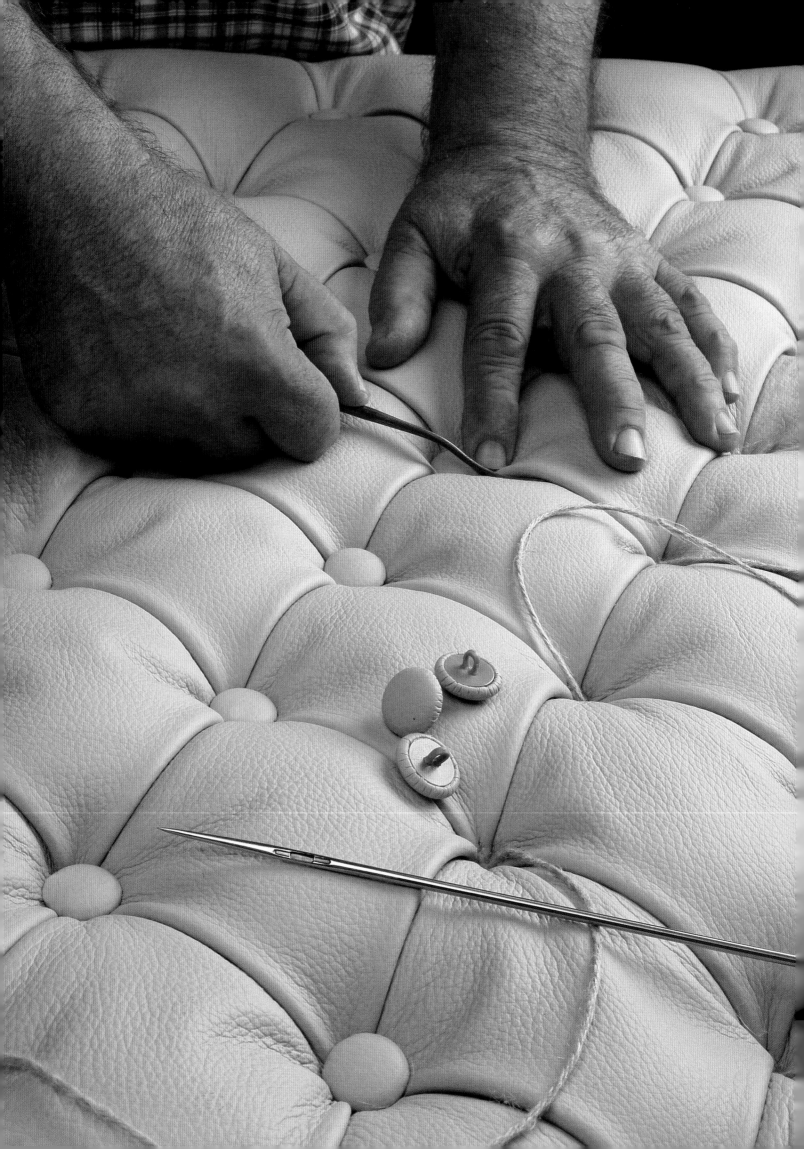

STEP
by Step

This chapter shows step by step and in detail the upholstering of various types of furniture. There are five different projects, and the processes are explained from the starting state of each piece of furniture to its finished upholstery.

These projects have been selected according to their level of difficulty so that each person can progress along with them while learning new skills. They also include specific solutions to common issues, complementing the information presented in the previous section. Together these two sections offer an in-depth look at the craft.

Reupholstered Chair

*T*his first step-by-step project shows the reupholstery process for the seat of a contemporary chair. It requires the complete replacement of the original upholstery. The covering, made of faux leather, shows cracks and small breaks. The webbing straps too are damaged, so it will be necessary to remove them and replace them with other materials.

In this case, the poor state of the structure of the seat has contributed to the deterioration of the faux leather covering. The project involves replacing the previous black seat with one of brown full-grain leather.

▼ **1.** This chair, made from stained wood, features a frame seat upholstered with webbing and a piece of latex foam; it sits on a wooden base which is attached to the furniture's frame.

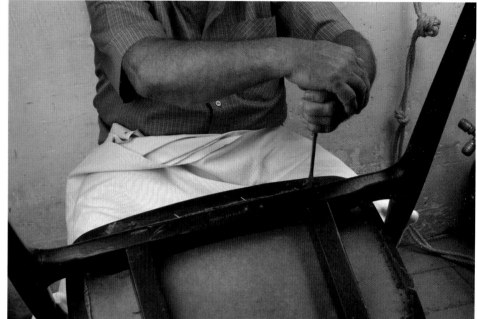

▲ **2.** The first step is to remove the old upholstery, which requires the removal of the seat. The chair is placed upside down and the seat is unscrewed from the frame.

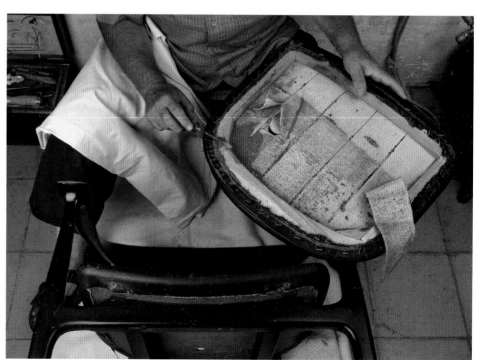

▶ **3.** Note that the webbing is broken and the latex foam appears to be in pretty bad shape.

▼ **4.** The wooden base that connects the seat to the frame is unscrewed. Keep the screws and washers for later.

▼ **5.** The staple/tack puller and pliers are used to extract the staples, and the piece of vinyl/synthetic leather which covered the base of the seat's structure is removed.

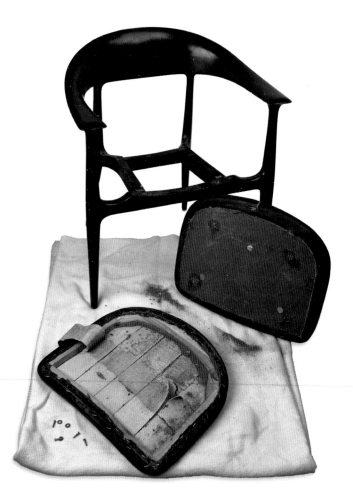

► **6.** Proceed likewise with the vinyl/synthetic leather finishing the edge and the seat. Note that the piece of latex foam is very deteriorated and has disintegrated into many pieces and dust.

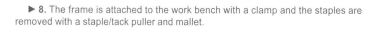

▲ **7.** The latex foam is removed from the webbing of the frame base using a scraper/palette knife. Then the webbing is cut with scissors.

► **8.** The frame is attached to the work bench with a clamp and the staples are removed with a staple/tack puller and mallet.

▼ **9.** It is necessary to remove all of the latex foam from the frame before re-upholstering. The remnants are softened by moistening them with a handful of cotton soaked with solvent.

▼ **10.** It is easily removed with a scraper.

► **11.** The frame is now perfectly clean and the wood is free of all traces of glue.

▲ **12.** Now the upholstery of the seat is mounted. Elastic webbing is used; first the vertical webbing is placed, from the front section to the rear in order to preserve the curvature of the seat. Measure the space within the frame and make sure you can place two webbing strips at each side with respect to the center line. They are stapled with ½-inch-wide (13 mm) staples, 80 (380) type, with a height of 9/16 inches (14 mm).

► **13.** Finally, three horizontal webbing strips are added by interweaving them with the vertical webbing.

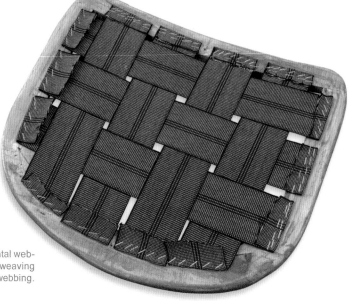

◄ 14. Polyurethane foam and padding is used for the seat. The frame is used as a template and placed onto the foam, and its outline is marked. In this case the foam has a density of 30 (30 kg/m3) and a thickness of 1¾₁₆ inches (3 cm). (Foam generally comes in whole-inch thicknesses, e.g., 1" to 6", but others may be special ordered.)

▼ 15. The piece is cut out with scissors.

◄ 16. Use a brush to evenly apply contact glue to the webbing.

► 17. The piece of polyurethane foam is perfectly centered on the frame and the entire surface is pressed to make sure it fully contacts the webbing.

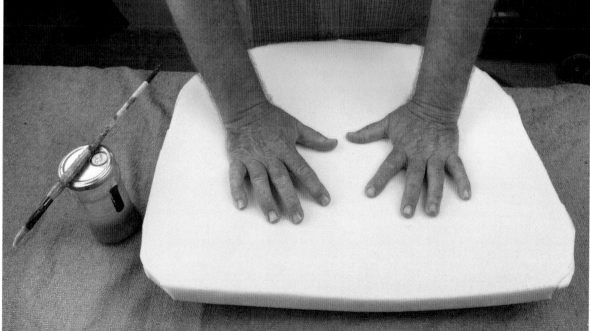

▶ **18.** Now the side edges of the foam piece are affixed to the frame. Contact glue is applied to the top half of one side of the piece of foam.

▶ **19.** It is glued to the top section of the frame so that the area with the glue is in contact with the wood and the aligned piece of foam.

▶ **20.** Start gluing from the center of each side and progress toward the sides.

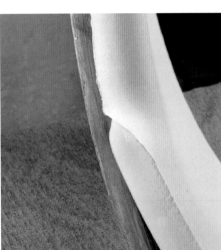

▲ **21.** The corners are also glued. The result: the foam is mounted on the wooden frame following the profile and the curvature of the seat.

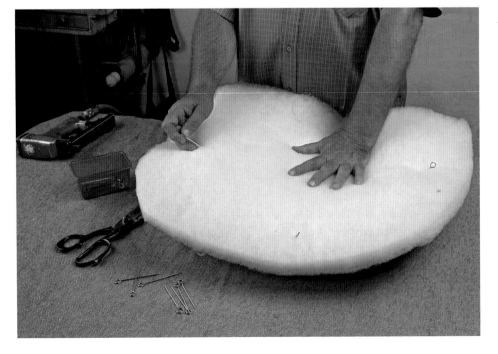

◀ **22.** Now a piece of batting is cut, somewhat larger than the seat because it will be affixed to the lower section of the frame. The area it will occupy at the lower section has been measured previously. The filling is placed centered on the foam and attached with several skewers to prevent it from slipping during the stapling process.

◀ **23.** The padding is attached to the lower section of the frame with the same size staples used earlier. Start stapling from the center of each of two opposite sides while smoothing the batting, and work in order toward the edges. The other two sides are stapled in the same way. The padding should not be stapled on the bottom of the frame, but near the bottom edge on all sides.

▼ **24.** View of the stapled filling. The extra material is cut off with scissors.

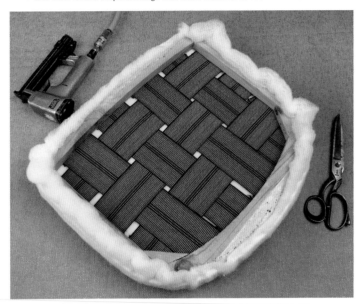

◀ **25.** Measure and cut a piece of brown full-grain leather, quite a bit larger than the seat. It is placed onto the seat, smoothed, and affixed with tacks to the bottom section of the frame starting at the front side. Once you are done it is stretched again; the tacks are removed from the front, and the leather is stretched and smoothed and affixed again with tacks.

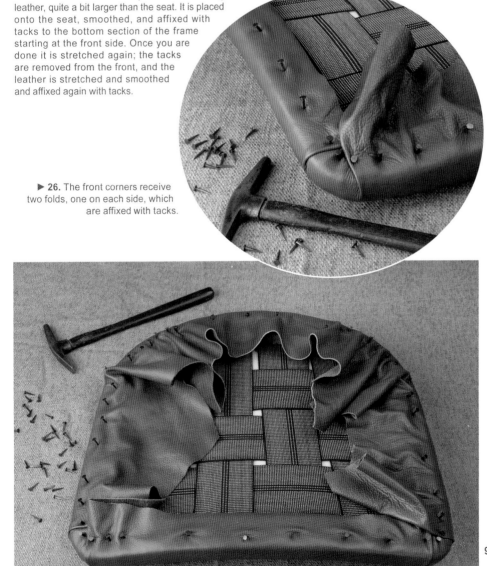

▶ **26.** The front corners receive two folds, one on each side, which are affixed with tacks.

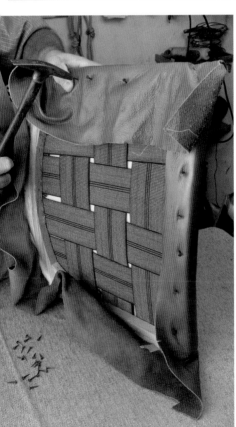

▶ **27.** View of the leather, pulled and smoothed and attached. The tacks keep the placement firm.

93

▼ **28.** Then the leather is stapled with ½-inch-wide (13 mm) staples, 80 (380) type, with a height of ⅜ inches (10 mm).

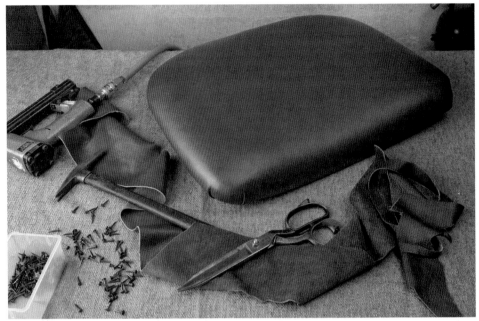

▲ **29.** The tacks are extracted with the upholsterer's hammer and the extra leather is cut back with scissors.

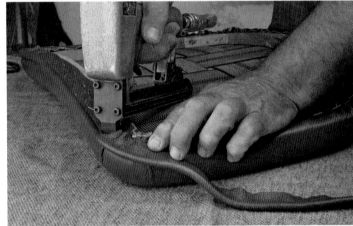

▲ **30.** The piping or cording made at the shop from the same leather as the seat is stapled to the frame using the same size staples. It must be aligned with the outer edge of the seat.

◄ **31.** Finally the exterior edge of the wood forming the base of the seat is covered with the same leather. Two pieces of leather are used and the seam between them is located at the rear section where it is invisible. Affix the leather temporarily with tacks and then use staples, just as before.

▼ **32.** View of the finished seat, ready to attach to the frame of the seat with the original screws.

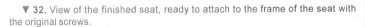

▼ **33.** The finished chair with new upholstery.

Dining Room Chair

This project teaches the process of upholstering a chair in its entirety, including the seat and the back rest. The structure of the furniture determines the type of upholstery; in this case it is composed of burlap and traditional stuffing, a simple upholstery and technically the easiest style. Manufactured piping is used for making the seat, which allows for quick progress.

▶ **1.** A common dining room chair from the 19th century made from varnished wood with bronze leg cups at the lower sections of the front legs.

◀ **2.** The first step is affixing the webbing. Jute webbing 3⅛ inches wide (8 cm) will be used. Mark the center section of the seat as well as the center edge of the frame (see page 52), and then the placement of the webbing is determined. It is affixed with ½-inch-long (12 mm) staples.

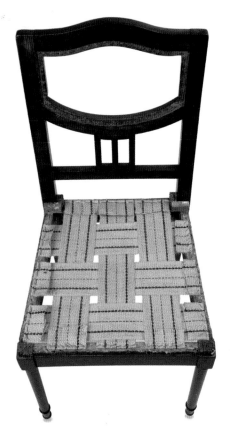

◀ **3.** The chair with three vertical straps of webbing and three interwoven horizontal straps.

▶ **4.** The burlap (a coffee bag) is placed on the webbing. The profile along the area of the back rest frame is cut with scissors to make it fit. It is affixed with staples, leaving extra burlap at all sides of the seat.

▲ **5.** Manufactured edge roll is used to make the sides of the seat. The piece is cut to the required size and the ends are wrapped with tape to prevent them from unraveling. Then they are firmly attached to the frame with tacks.

▲ **6.** The extra burlap is folded up and over the edge roll toward the lower section and affixed with staples to the frame, right next to it.

◄ **7.** Proceed the same way with the other sides of the seat, folding the edging at a right angle at the two front corners.

► **8.** View of the finished process. Note that the burlap has been stapled around its interior perimeter as have the center sections of the angles of the front corners.

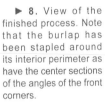

◄ **9.** Then the ties are added horizontally (see page 57) at the interior perimeter and vertically with long basting stitches using the semicircular needle.

◄ **10.** The first layer of filling is done using vegetable fiber (see page 58).

97

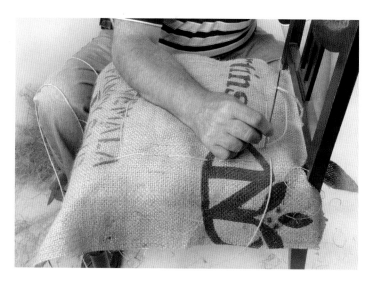

◄ **11.** Now a new piece of burlap is placed onto the filling and affixed to the seat with a top stitch (see page 59), this time with the double-pointed needle.

► **12.** Once the stitching is done, the thread is tightened by pulling it taut at each baste. To make sure the stitches are done correctly the burlap has been marked with tailor's chalk.

◄ **13.** Once the top stitching is complete, the burlap is stapled to the frame of the seat.

► **14.** A regulator is used to adjust the filling and to distribute it uniformly in the areas close to the edging. Try to avoid leaving any areas without filling near the edging.

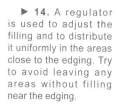

► **15.** The basted stitches on the top are slightly loosened and will provide the ties for the top filling. Once the process is done, the end of the thread is knotted.

► **16.** Coconut filling or horsehair is used for the second filling layer; this is a high-quality filling which provides a good texture to the seat.

◄ 17. A piece of batting of density 300 is cut, slightly larger than the seat. It is placed centered on it and affixed with skewers, folding the ends toward the inside. Note that the profile of the back rest frame has been cut out. The areas at the front corners are also cut to keep the filling from being too thick.

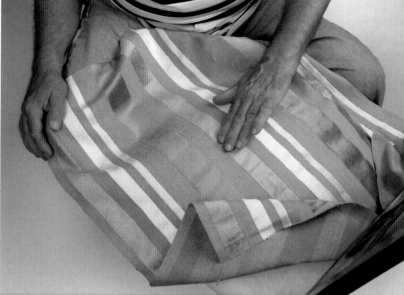

▲ 18. The piece of fabric for the covering of the seat, in this case featuring a velvet striped motif, is cut. Check the grain of the fabric (see page 70): on the seats the fabric is always placed with the grain going from the rear to the front; in the case of arm rests, it is placed with the grain going from the top down.

◄ 19. Then it is centered on the seat based on the two gray lines (the widest ones) so that one of the sides of the white strip is aligned with the center. The fabric is affixed with skewers. Tacks are not used, as this is a simple type of upholstery which does not require a lot of stretching of the fabric.

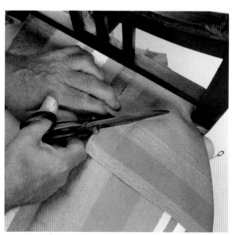

◄ ▶ 20. Then the covering fabric is adjusted to fit the profile of the back rest frame. First a diagonal cut up to about ⅜ inch (1 cm) from the wood is made without reaching it, then another vertical cut (parallel to the front of the back rest) is made about 9/16 to ¾ inch (1.5 to 2 cm) from it in order to later fold the fabric toward the inside.

◀ **21.** The fabric is stapled to the frame; start at the rear section and move from the center to the edges. The fabric is stretched and smoothed from the rear to the front and stapled as well. The sides are stapled without pulling the fabric but by gently following them; otherwise the stripes might become skewed. The area in front of the back rest is also stapled.

▼ **22.** The two corners are given a vertical fold. First a vertical cut is made up to the area where the fabric will be affixed to the frame.

▲ **23.** The fabric is stapled to the wood of the frame right over the previous cut.

▶ **24.** Next, a new horizontal cut is made up to the end of the white stripe and the extra fabric is cut off.

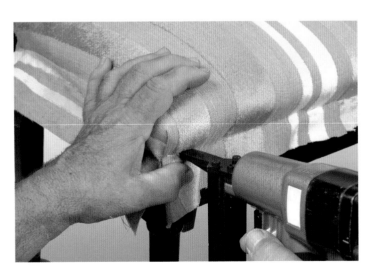

▲ **25.** A vertical fold toward the inside is made and the front fabric is folded over the first staple. Then it is stapled.

▶ **26.** The extra fabric is cut off with a razor cutter just below the line of staples; try to avoid marking the wood. Be careful not to cut into the secured fabric above the staples.

◄ ◄ 27. The next step is to upholster the back rest. Measure the rear section of the back rest, cut the piece of fabric that will make up the covering, and affix it with staples. Note that the pattern repeats the seat pattern—make sure that the stripes are aligned with each other.

► 28. The fabric for the rear section is attached from the inside of the frame with staples. Then a piece of batting of density 100 is cut to the size of the interior of the back rest and placed onto the fabric.

► 29. Proceed as you did with the burlap: cut one piece, fold it under along its entire perimeter, and staple it to the interior of the frame, pulling it taut.

► 30. The ties of the burlap are made with thread and the curved needle to secure the stuffing.

► 31. Coconut filling is used here as well.

101

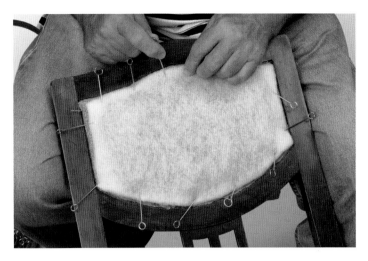

▲ 32. A piece of batting of density 100 similar to the previous piece is cut and the filling is covered. Skewers are used to affix it in a perfectly centered position.

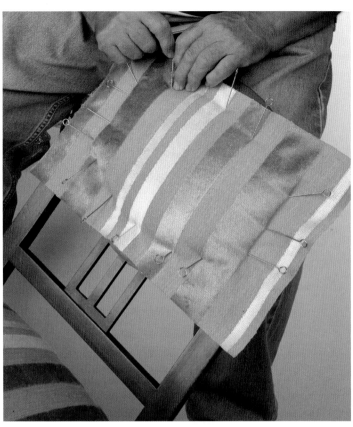

▶ 33. Now the front of the back rest is measured, and the corresponding covering fabric is cut. Just as in the previous example (see step 27) it is made corresponding to the centered motif of the seat, with a similar alignment of the stripes. It is placed centered on the seat while removing the filling-holding skewers one by one and sticking them back into the complete assembly, to temporarily affix the fabric.

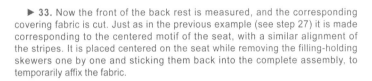

◀ 34. The fabric is stapled from the center toward the sides.

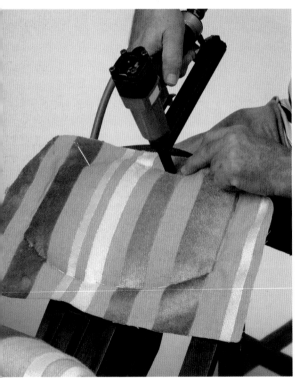

▶ 35. Once again the extra fabric is cut away with a cutter following a process similar to the one used for the seat. The section is finished with braid and cord which is affixed using hot glue. Work carefully and avoid letting the glue stain the fabric or the braid. Tip: cover the inside back fabric with a scrap piece of fabric for protection.

▶ 36. To finish the project, a piece of sturdy white fabric is placed on the bottom section of the seat. Measure and cut a piece with the same dimensions, and staple it. Next, make a diagonal cut into the fabric at the inside corner of each leg. Finally, fold under the raw edge and staple in place.

▶ 37. The finished chair.

Armchair

*T*his step-by-step project shows the processes involved in upholstering a French armchair from the 19th century. The fabric covering has some damage and the seat has lost its firmness, so the entire piece must be taken apart. While disassembling the chair, it becomes obvious that the back rest is in good shape, so that will not need to be taken apart. The original's center back furrow requires reupholstering the armchair with various sections sewn together; the fabric of this element will be affixed to the frame using braces. It will be necessary to sew the covering of the front finish of the arm rests, and also to sew the rear section to secure it. This armchair will have a fixed seat.

► **1.** View of the armchair. Notice the bad condition of the covering fabric and some finishing elements such as the trim at the arm rests, and the deteriorated firmness of the seat.

◄ **2.** The chair is disassembled starting at the bottom section of the chair. The webbing is completely useless.

▼ **3.** While taking apart the chair, the back rest turns out to be in good condition and is therefore not replaced.

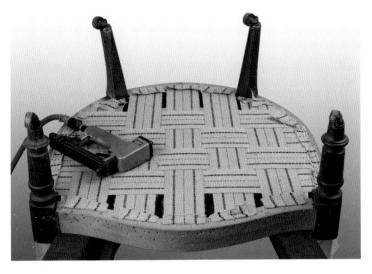

▲ **4.** The first step is to affix the new webbing to the bottom section of the seat. These are jute webbing strips with a width of 3⅛ inches (8 cm). Measure and mark the center of the seat (see page 52) and attach the webbing with 9⁄16-inch-long (14 mm) staples.

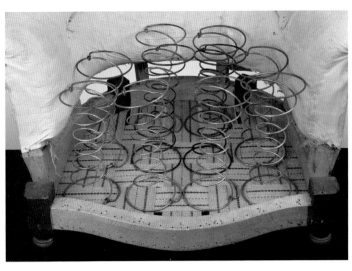

▲ **5.** For the seat we use soft springs with 7 turns. They are placed with the top knot at the "ten to ..." position (as if it were the face of a clock) in two rows of four at the front and center, and a line of two springs at the rear as shown. Then the webbing is sewn (see page 54).

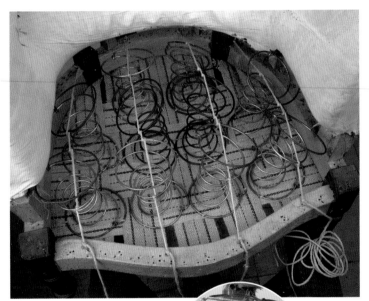

◄ **6.** The springs are first tied at the rear section of the seat, working forward and using simple knots (see page 56). Then return to the rear section making double knots.

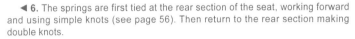

▼ **7.** Now the horizontal ties are done. The placement of the front horizontal line of the springs coincides with the arm rest brace so it requires a special attaching method. The cord is affixed to the wood of the frame with tacks to both sides of the brace, and the end of the cord is passed through the inside of the tie.

► **8.** Then the springs are tied at their third turn or loop. This keeps the springs in place and reinforces the structure.

► **9.** The diagonal ties are done with a double knot (see page 56). View of the finished structure.

▶ **10.** Now the burlap is placed onto the set of tied springs and stitched (see page 57). Then the frame of the seat is stapled with height of ⁹⁄₁₆ inch (14-mm) staples. Make the ties at the top and front sections of the seat.

▼ **11.** The first layer of filling is done with palm fibers.

▶ **12.** A new piece of burlap is placed on it and stitched using the top stitch (see page 59).

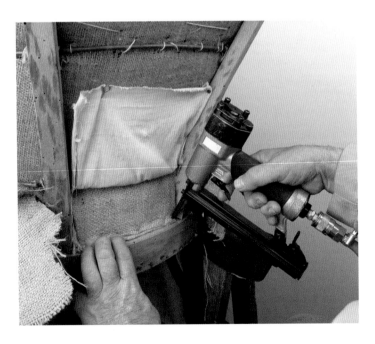

◀ **13.** When finished the burlap is passed to the rear section of the chair to adequately affix it to the frame; two cuts are made coinciding with each of the back rest braces. This helps to adjust the burlap correctly, and it is then stapled to the wooden frame with staples of the same size as those used before.

▶ **14.** Now the ladder stitch is done (see page 60) to shape and emphasize the frontal contour of the seat. The ties that hold the filling are padded with coconut fiber filling to assure a fluffy consistency.

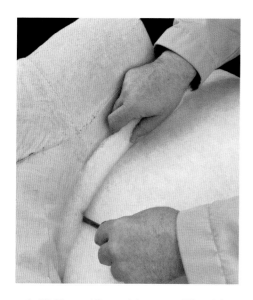

◄ **15.** Then the seat is measured and a piece of batting of density 300 is cut, slightly larger than the seat. It is placed on the filling, running the ends between the braces of the back rest up to the rear section of the frame; it helps to use a screwdriver or other long tool such as a strip of wood.

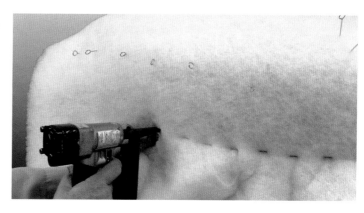

▲ **16.** Skewers are used to affix the batting, which is then stapled to the frame with staples similar to those used previously. Make sure the batting is pulled and smoothed perfectly. The extra material is cut off with scissors.

► **17.** Measure the seat (see page 69) and then measure and mark the covering piece, which in this case consists of fabric. It is centered on a flower motif, and the cut lines are marked with tailor's chalk on the right side of the fabric.

▼ **18.** The piece of fabric is place centered onto the seat using the central motif as a guide. Measure the width of the seat and mark its center as well as the motif's center with a skewer. Center it with respect to the front and rear part of the seat as well.

► ► **19.** The next step is to pass the rear section of the fabric to the rear of the armchair. Since the back rest consists of braces it will be necessary to make cuts so the piece will be placed correctly. It helps to place a piece of flat wood next to the brace. It will act as a ruler or guide to make the cut which will reach up to 1³⁄₁₆ inches (3 cm) from the brace; make another diagonal cut as well. Proceed the same way for all of the sides of the frame braces.

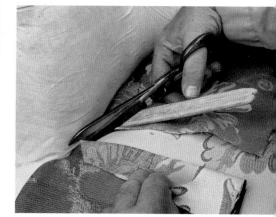

► **20.** The fabric is passed to the rear part of the armchair using a piece of wood.

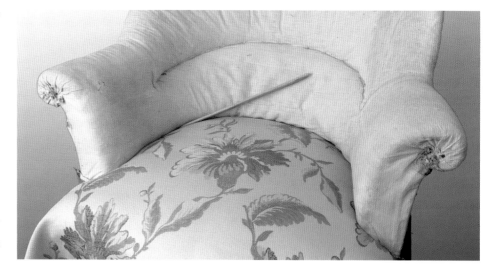

▼ **21.** The fabric is stapled to the frame. It is attached to the braces or the legs with two opposing folds. The center section is stitched and the fabric at both sides is left loose to make the folds.

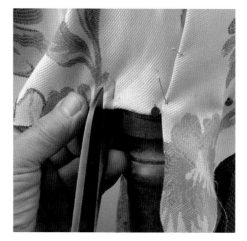

▲ **22.** Now the fabric to be placed below the fold is attached with a staple. Make a cut to assure a perfect fold.

▲ **23.** The fabric is stapled to the frame and the folds are affixed with pins.

◄ ◄ **24.** Then the two folds are sewn with a small curved needle and nylon thread. Small alternating stitches are made along both sides of the fold while removing the pins.

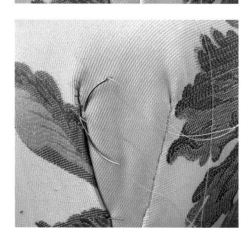

▲ **25.** The fabric of the lower section of the folds is attached to the frame using finishing staples. Then the lateral part is stapled to the frame (the lower section of the arm rest) with similar staples. This is done because the area will be covered by the fabric used to upholster the outside of the armchair. The rest is stapled to the frame as well.

▼ **26.** Then the central section of the back rest is measured and marked, even though it had a previous mark on the original). Check that the center mark is equidistant to the beginning of the arm rests and that it coincides with the seam of the fabric that covers the original filling.

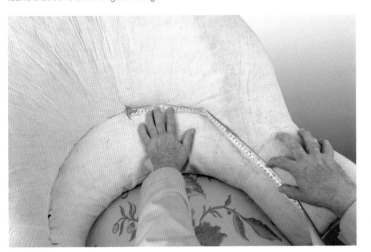

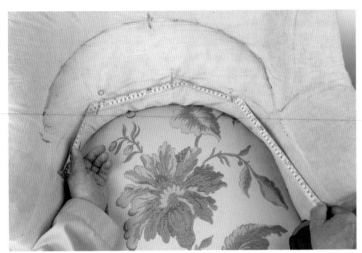

▶ **31.** The piece of fabric is placed centered on the section of the lower back support and affixed with skewers. The furrow is marked with tailor's chalk.

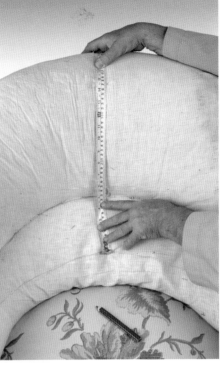

◀ **27.** Mark the central section of the semicircle that will be part of the lower section of the back rest with a pencil. Check to ensure that the placement is matching the proportions of the back rest, that is, that the distance from the line to the upper section of the back rest is double the distance of that from the line to the lower section.

◀ **28.** Measure the total width at the central part, just above the mark.

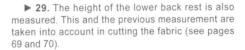

▶ **29.** The height of the lower back rest is also measured. This and the previous measurement are taken into account in cutting the fabric (see pages 69 and 70).

◀ **30.** To adjust the repetition of the fabric patterns of the back rest to match those of the seat, the area between two flowers is chosen to center the piece. Just as with the seat, the piece of fabric (in this case 11¹³⁄₁₆ x 27⁹⁄₁₆ inches / 30 x 70 cm) is marked with tailor's chalk and is cut following the lines.

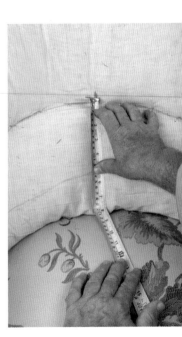

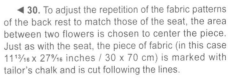

► **33.** Now the measurements of the fabric piece that will conform the upholstering of the rest of the back rest—in this case, 23 ⅝ x 35⁷⁄₁₆ inches (60 x 90 cm)—are taken. The piece is centered around one of the flowers which will be in a position reflecting that of the seat. Mark it and place it onto the armchair at the desired position, and affix it with skewers. Use tailor's chalk to mark the upper limit of the lower section of the back rest.

► **34.** Once again the extra fabric below the line is cut off, leaving a margin of about ¾ inch (2 cm).

▼ **35.** The pieces are taken down. Then the shape of the piece that will be used to upholster the lower section of the back rest is made symmetric: it is folded at the center section and cut.

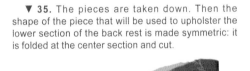

▲ **36.** The process is the same for the piece of fabric that will be used to upholster the top section of the seat; it has been previously marked at the lower center.

► **37.** The pieces are assembled with the two center marks as a reference, and secured with pins. The seam is machine-sewn with nylon thread.

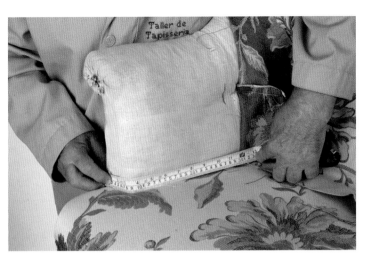

◀ **38.** Take the measurement of the arm rest (see page 69). You need a piece of fabric 15¾ x 11¹³⁄₁₆ inches (40 x 30 cm) for each of them. They too are centered based on a floral motif. Mark them just as in previous examples.

▶ **39.** After stapling the fabric of the seat one of the pieces of 15¾ x 11¹³⁄₁₆ inches (40 x 30 cm) is placed onto an arm rest.

▼ **40.** Skewers are used to affix the piece, based on the position of the central motif.

▲ **41.** The ends of the two pieces of fabric that will make up the back rest upholstery are folded where the arm rest begins. Another fold is made with the piece of fabric of the arm rest, at the same area. The two folds are pinned together and the extra fabric is cut off, leaving an edge similar to those of previous steps.

◀ **42.** The fabric of the back rest will be trimmed at the lower section with piping, and is secured to the frame with a strap. For this reason the placement for the piping is marked with tailor's chalk following the lower profile of the back rest.

◄ 43. The entire fabric covering is removed from the armchair and placed onto the work bench. Following the process used previously, the extra fabric of the lower section of the lower back support's semicircle is cut.

► 44. The covering is dismantled and the pins holding the pieces together are removed. Then the back rest piece is folded at the center and the extra fabric is cut off.

◄ ◄ 45. Use the already cut and adjusted piece of arm rest fabric as a template to cut the piece of fabric to be used to upholster the other arm rest. The lower piece is cut using the top piece as a guide.

◄ 46. This process assures that the section consisting of the four pieces of fabric that make up the back rest and arm rests will be symmetrical, as will the seams between them. Then the section is sewn.

► 47. Now the section is laid out on the armchair and checked for proper fit. Then a piece of piping is made, in this case approximately 1½ yards (1.3 m) long, from the upholstery fabric and is affixed to the lower part of the section. Finally the strap is sewn (see page 71).

▶ **48.** A piece of batting of density 300 is cut slightly larger than the back rest and arm rests, and affixed with skewers, especially at the furrow line.

▼ **49.** Then the batting is sewn at the furrow line with a top stitch (see page 59) using normal thread. A curved needle is used here, although a straight double-pointed needle can also be utilized.

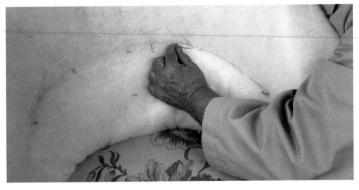

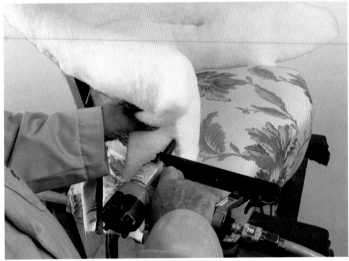

▶ **50.** Once the furrow has been sewn, the batting is attached to the rear section of the frame using staples. Special attention is paid to make sure it is perfectly smoothed and pulled snugly, and the extra fabric is cut off with scissors.

▶ **51.** The fold at the front section of the arm rest is cut and the batting is sewn with normal thread and a straight stitch.

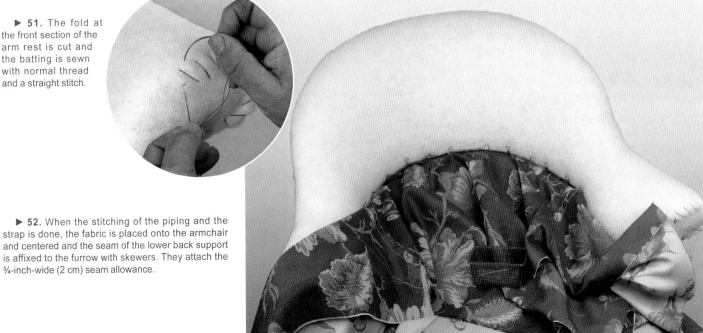

▶ **52.** When the stitching of the piping and the strap is done, the fabric is placed onto the armchair and centered and the seam of the lower back support is affixed to the furrow with skewers. They attach the ¾-inch-wide (2 cm) seam allowance.

113

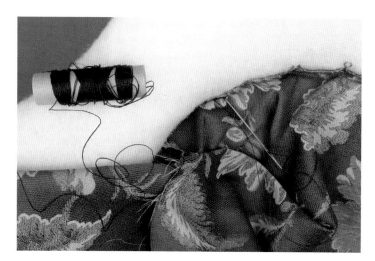

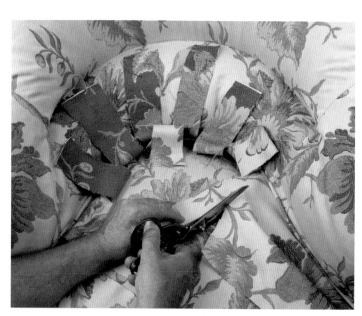

◄ 53. The fabric is stitched to the back rest with a blind stitch and red upholstery thread, matching the reverse side.

▼ 54. Then the rest of the fabric is affixed with skewers. Note that the fabric is perfectly centered on the back rest and the arm rests of the armchair.

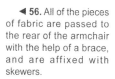

◄ 55. Now the strap is passed to the rear section of the furniture to attach the upholstery fabric to the frame. Various vertical cuts are made in the fabric to facilitate the correct fit of the piece against the curvature of the back rest, but excluding the piping.

◄ 56. All of the pieces of fabric are passed to the rear of the armchair with the help of a brace, and are affixed with skewers.

► 57. The arm rests at their front section receive folds; first they are affixed with skewers to the area where the folds are made and with tacks at the lower section. The piping is also temporarily secured with tacks.

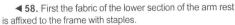

◄ 58. First the fabric of the lower section of the arm rest is affixed to the frame with staples.

► 59. Then the folds of the arm rest are made and stapled to the lower section of the frame.

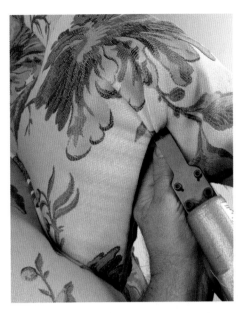

▼ 60. Once all of the folds except the last one have been made, the fabric of the arm rests and the back rest is affixed with the same size staples. To perfectly adjust the fabric to the curved profile of the arm rest, a few vertical cuts are made, without reaching to the tacked area. This allows you to smooth and pull each piece individually and to adjust the fabric to the shape of the furniture.

► 61. The last fold of the front section of the arm rest is made and affixed with pins. Then the fabric is stapled to the frame making sure that the folds on both sides of the armchair are symmetrical.

► 62. The last fold is sewn with white nylon thread and a curved needle, using small stitches. This adds the final touch and prevents the folds from opening.

► 63. Now the rear of the armchair is fitted. The extra fabric of the straps, which had been stapled to the frame, is cut off and the fabric that covers the original filling of the back rest and the burlap is sewn with a double-pointed needle and normal thread using wide stitches.

◀ **64.** The piping that will be used to finish the rear section of the armchair (see page 71) is made, and is slightly longer than the required length, in this case 98⅞ inches (250 cm). The center of the piece is marked and positioned so that the successive seams of the fabric will be equidistant (several pieces were required to make the piping).

▲ **65.** The piping is attached with staples just below the rear curvature of the back rest and continued to the lower section of the arm rests to trim their edges. To attach the end of the piping to the lower section of the frame, the fabric that will be affixed is unstitched and the extra core is removed from it.

▲ **66.** Then it is stapled to the frame.

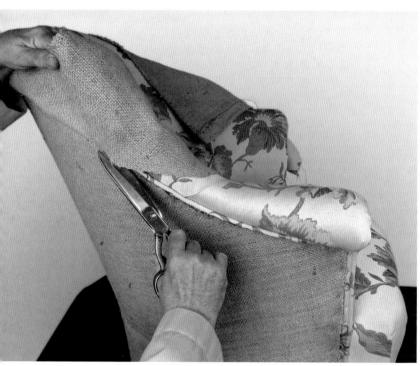

▲ **67.** Now the process is repeated at the rear of the armchair. A piece of perfectly pulled burlap is stapled and the extra fabric is cut off. The original filling was horsehair, and it has been replaced with batting.

▶ **68.** A piece of batting of density 100 is cut slightly larger than the rear section of the armchair and stapled to the frame, then the extra fabric is cut off. The piece of fabric (also slightly larger than the rear) is placed, perfectly centered, and affixed with skewers.

▲ **69.** The skewers are placed all around the perimeter about ¾ inch (2 cm) above the piping. Once it has been attached the extra fabric is cut off ⅜ inch (1 cm) above the piping.

▲ **70.** Then the fabric is folded under and tacked just below the piping.

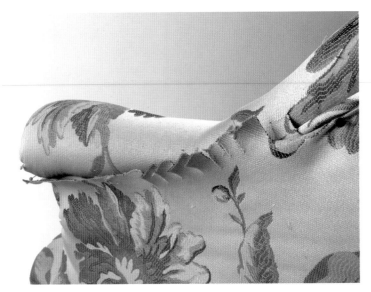

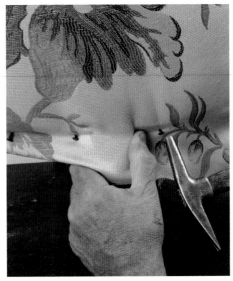

◄ **72.** Once the top and lateral sections of the arm rests are affixed, proceed likewise with the lower section, make sure that the fabric is perfectly tensioned.

▲ **71.** To make sure that the fabric is perfectly adjusted to the lower curvature of the arm rests, several vertical cuts are made. They should never reach the point where the fold is. If you don't work this way the contour of the fold will not be smooth and the fabric will form creases. The fabric is folded under and affixed with tacks.

◄◄ **73.** The fabric covering the rear section of the armchair is attached to the piping by sewing it with white nylon thread (so as to make the seam invisible) using a small curved needle. First a vertical stitch through the interior of the rear fabric is made, and then the needle is run below the piping.

▶▶ **74.** Do the same on the other side: first a vertical stitch is made through the interior of the fabric, and then passed under the piping.

▼ **75.** The entire perimeter is sewn following the previous process.

▼ **76.** The section where the fabric meets the rear legs is handled by making a vertical cut and two diagonal cuts (without reaching the top section of the leg). Then the center section is folded toward the inside and affixed with a tack; the two horizontal sections of the fabric are stapled to the lower part of the frame. The center section will be attached with trimming stitches similar to the fabric at the front feet.

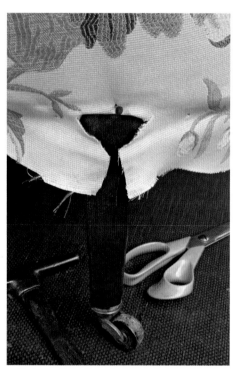

▶ **77.** The fabric is stapled to the lower section of the frame. To finish the task a piece of sturdy white fabric is affixed, perfectly smoothed and stretched.

▼ **78.** The finished armchair.

Antique Sofa

*T*his project shows the processes involved in completely upholstering an antique sofa. In this case the traditional upholstery processes are applied, with the aim being to recover the piece of furniture after restoring its frame. The piece consists of only its frame. The sofa has a fixed seat and its back rest is made with a center furrow, following the upholstery styles and characteristics that were common to the sofa's era. The fabric is affixed to the frame with braces. These processes serve to complement those that were explained in the "Technical Processes" section.

◄ **1.** The frame of this sofa is made from pine wood with a few pieces of solid mahogany at the legs and the top of the back rest, and mahogany veneer on the other elements. It dates from the 19th century, and is Isabel-style from northern Europe. The carpentry restoration has strengthened its structure and varnish has been applied. After the upholstering is finished a new coat of varnish will be applied.

▲ **2.** Jute webbing with a width of 3⅛ inches (8 cm) is used. The three parts into which the seat is divided (indicated by crossbeam braces) are measured and marked. It is possible to place four webbing strips across each seat section. Use a marker to mark the central section of the lower part of the frame. That will serve as a guide for attaching the ends of the webbing (see page 52). Note that the webbing at the edges along the line between the rear and the front legs is affixed from the rear to the front, the reverse of the others. They are stapled with ⅝-inch-high (16 mm) staples.

▲ **3.** Then the lengthwise webbing is affixed the same way (see page 53).

► **4.** To secure and reinforce the piece, a folded length of webbing is placed over the brace and affixed with staples.

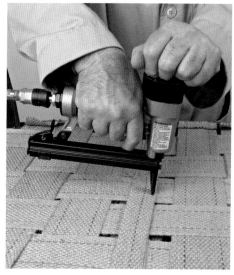

▼ **5.** The sofa is placed right side up onto two sawhorses, and the springs are placed uniformly onto the base and the crossbeams. These are original and high-quality springs with 13 turns, which is higher than currently-available springs, and they match the structure and the characteristics of the sofa. They are all placed in the same position with the knot of the final turn in the "ten to ..." clock position.

► **6.** They are stitched at the bottom ring or turn to the webbing using three stitches of four-stranded thread. Try to keep the springs in the correct position throughout the process.

► **7.** The springs are attached wtith U nails on the crossbeams, using the upholsterer's hammer.

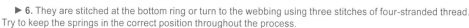

► ► **8.** A piece of thick fabric is placed on the crossbeam braces to keep the springs from squeaking when they touch the wood when the furniture is sat on. Run it through the inside of the lower rings of the springs and staple it.

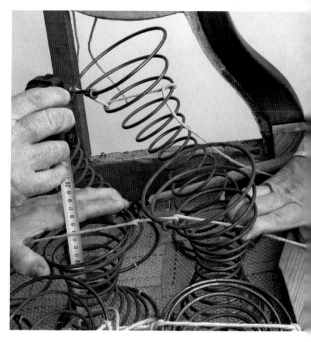

► **9.** Now the springs are tied (see page 57). Given the fact that these are high springs they must be set at a height of 5½ inches (14 cm). This may require two people working together to check the height with a tape measure.

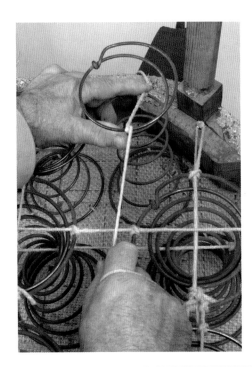

◄ 10. The springs are tied with simple knots both horizontally and vertically. Finally the springs are tied from the rear section of the seat where the frame curves, which is not aligned with the vertical ties.

▼ 11. View of the set of springs with the finished horizontal and vertical ties. (The spring at the rear section has been tied horizontally to the springs with which it has been aligned while no vertical ties have been made to any of the springs.)

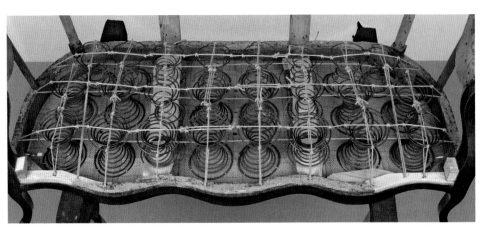

► 12. Then the diagonal ties of the springs are made with double knots (see page 58).

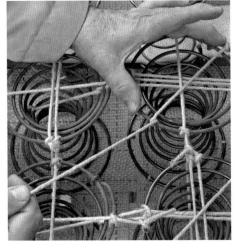

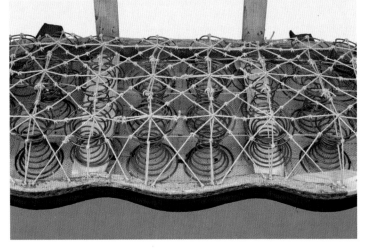

▲ 13. The finished springs and ties.

◄ 14. Check whether the set of the springs is comfortable and ensure that the springs do not squeak, by sitting down on it.

▶ **15.** The next part of the process involves cutting a piece of burlap (in this case a coffee bag) slightly larger in size than the seat. It is placed over the set of springs, and sewn to them and affixed to the frame with ⁹⁄₁₆ inch (14-mm) staples. The extra fabric is cut off and the ties are made (see page 57).

▼ **16.** Now the first layer of filling is done (see page 58) using palm fibers. The first layer of filling will be secured under the ties and will form an even layer across the burlap base.

◀ **17.** The second step is to place the second piece of burlap and affix it with tacks.

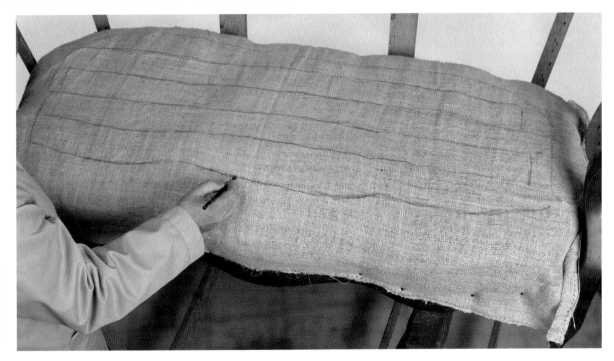

▶ **18.** Tailor's chalk is used to mark the placement of the top stitching, separated from the front of the seat by three to four fingers' width.

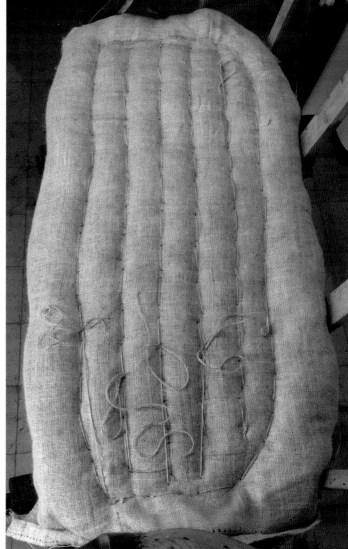

▲ **19.** The top stitch is used (see page 59), first along the outside edge and then on the inside of the seat following the marks. The top stitches are some three fingers wide, and the lower stitch is about one finger wide. While stitching, pull the thread taut to secure the filling.

▶ **20.** View of the finished top stitch and the pulled thread. The filling is perfectly attached and secured.

▲ **21.** Next, the burlap is stapled to the frame with staples of similar size as used before. First the burlap is stapled to the rear section of the seat; start at the center and proceed to the sides, pulling it taut as you progress. Then the sides and the front are done, from the center toward the sides while tensioning.

▶ **22.** The filling is positioned to obtain the desired thickness and placement by using the regulator's pointed end to move it.

◄ 23. The front of the seat is finished by shaping and emphasizing the contour with a ladder stitch (see page 60).

► 24. Then the ties of the top burlap are made and the second filling layer, consisting of coconut fibers or horsehair, is done. The resulting surface is fluffy and has a comfortable feel.

► 25. A piece of batting of density 300 is cut, slightly larger than the seat, and then affixed with skewers. The extra fabric is cut off.

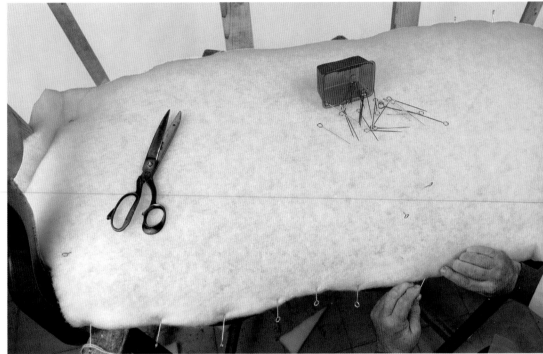

▼ 26. The pieces of batting that will cover the front part of the seat are also cut and affixed with skewers.

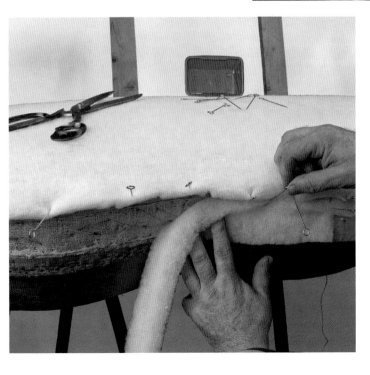

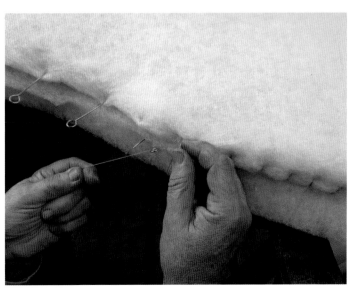

▲ 27. The lower burlap and the two pieces of batting are sewn with nylon thread and an upholsterer's needle. Both pieces are sewn at the same time.

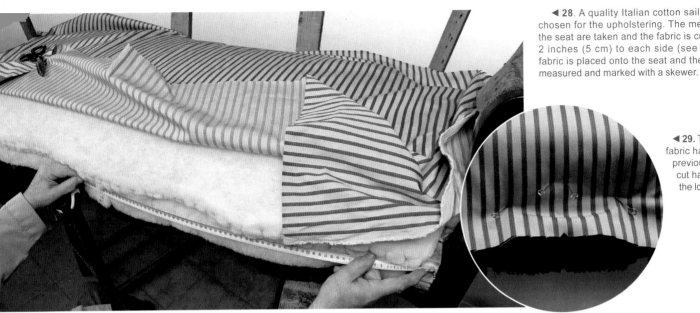

◄ 28. A quality Italian cotton sailcloth has been chosen for the upholstering. The measurements of the seat are taken and the fabric is cut adding about 2 inches (5 cm) to each side (see page 70). The fabric is placed onto the seat and the front center is measured and marked with a skewer.

◄ 29. The center of the fabric has been marked previously and a small cut has been made at the lower section.

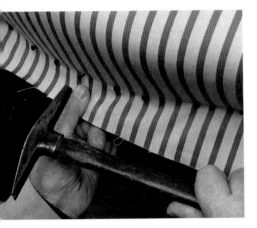

◄ 30. The fabric is affixed to the frame with tacks, first the front section and then moving in sequence toward the sides.

► 31. Proceed the same way at the backs of the sides, tensioning the fabric so that the stripes are straight. Two cuts are made where the seat meets the back rest frame to ensure the correct placement of the fabric.

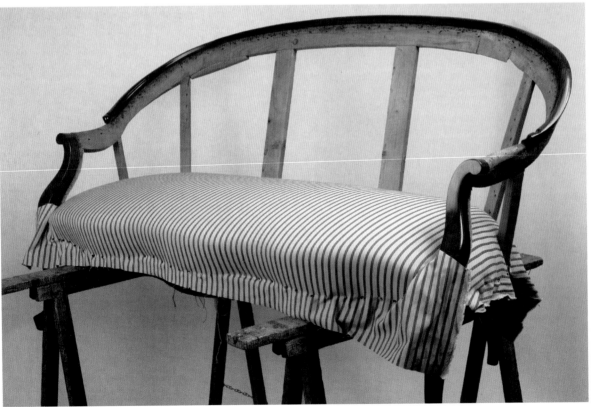

◄ 32. The finished affixed fabric. Check that the stripes are straight and that each side edge's patterning matches. In this case the sides end with a strawberry-colored stripe.

◄ 33. Then the fabric is affixed with ½ inch (12-mm) staples; start at the center front and proceed in order toward the sides. Extract the tacks with the tack puller, and staple.

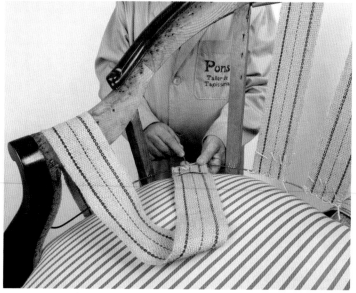

▲ **34.** The fabric is affixed along the frame of the arm rest.

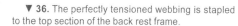

◄ 35. The back rest is made with webbing. A lower cross beam is fashioned with steel wire, and placed about one finger's width away from the seat. It is attached with metal fasteners to the frame and the rear part of the arm rests. Then the webbing is affixed to the wire, sewing it with a double-pointed needle.

▼ **36.** The perfectly tensioned webbing is stapled to the top section of the back rest frame.

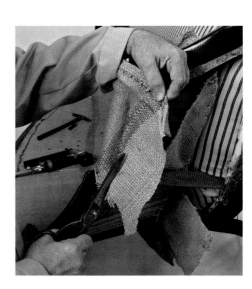

◀ **37.** The section is covered with burlap; it is sewn to the webbing at its lower section and affixed to the wooden frame with staples.

▶ **38.** Note that a few cuts have been made at the lower section of the burlap to facilitate its adjustment and to be able to pass it to the rear part of the back rest to be attached. The area around the arm rests is also stapled.

▶ **39.** A piece of cloth is placed on the seat to protect the upholstery from possible damage. The ties on the burlap are stitched and the first filling layer is done with palm fibers (see page 58). The second burlap is placed on the back rest and the arm rest (one piece each) and affixed with skewers. The location of the central furrow (lumbar section) is marked with a pencil.

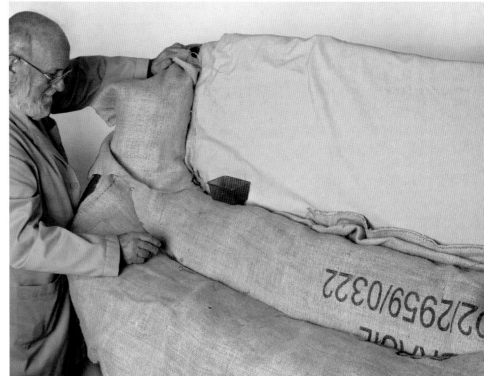

▼ **40.** The furrow is sewn following the marked line with a top stitch (see page 59) using a double-pointed needle; the thread exits from the rear section of the seat and connects the burlap and the webbing.

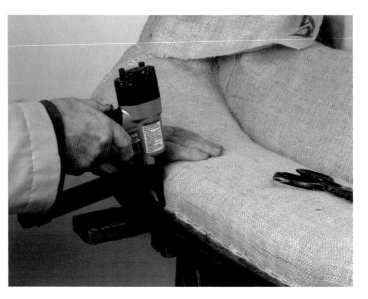

◀ **41.** The burlap is cut and stapled to the frame about ¾ inch (2 cm) from the top finishing piece of the seat. As usual, start at the center and proceed toward the sides.

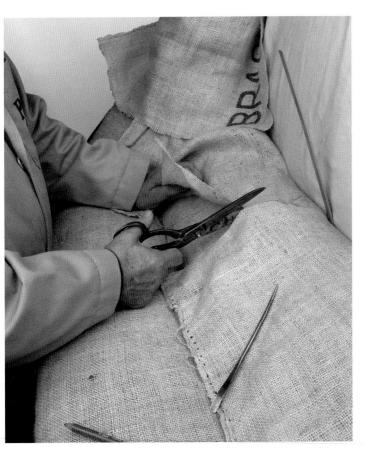

◄ **42.** Once the top part of the burlap has been attached, the lower part is passed under the back rest. A few cuts are made at the braces of the seat.

▼ **43.** A metal rod (or a wooden strip) is used to insert the burlap between the back rest and the seat passing it to the rear section of the frame.

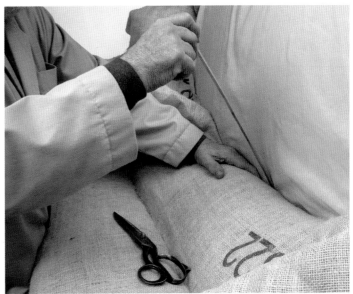

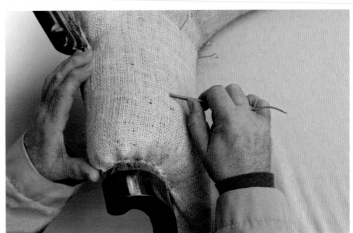

▲ **44.** The pieces of burlap that will cover the arm rests are also stapled to the frame and they are affixed with skewers where they meet the burlap of the seat.

▲ **45.** The regulator tool is used to adjust the volume and placement of the filling in the arm and back rests.

► **46.** The burlap of the arm rests is sewn to the inside back burlap with an upholsterer's needle and both arm rests are finished with a blind stitch first, then with a piping stitch (see page 60).

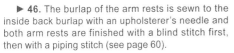

▲ **47.** The top and the bottom filling of the back rest is attached at the rear section and the extra fabric is cut off.

▲ **48.** Both perfectly stretched pieces of burlap are affixed to the webbing with skewers and sewn with the upholsterer's needle.

▶ **49.** Then the top finishing of the back rest is done with a ladder stitch.

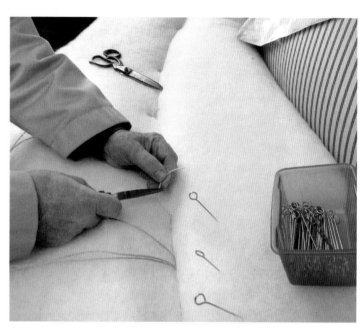

▲ **50.** A piece of batting of density 300 is cut and placed over the back rest, the central furrow is affixed with skewers, and the burlap is sewn with straight stitches. In some cases it might be difficult to pass the needle and thread through the assembly consisting of batting, the fabrics, and the filling, so pliers may come in handy to pull it.

◀ **51.** Once the furrow of the batting has been sewn a second filling layer is made at the back rest. This will only be a partial filling for the lower part of the back, to provide comfort. Proceed as before: first the ties are made and then the filling layer of palm fiber is added. Then it is covered with batting and affixed with skewers.

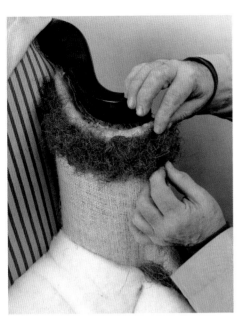

▲ 52. The second filling layer is made for both arm rests, proceeding as in previous steps.

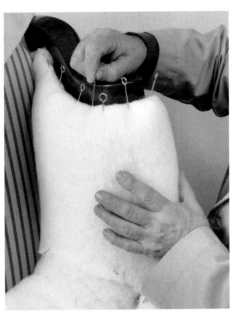

▲ 53. Two pieces of batting of density 300 are cut and placed onto the arm rests of the sofa. The extra fabric is cut off, and they are affixed with skewers.

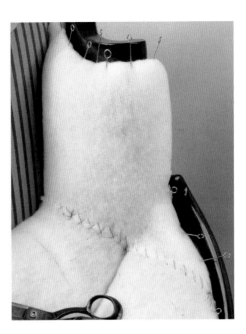

▲ 54. They are sewn to the batting of the back rest with whip stitches and the upholsterer's needle.

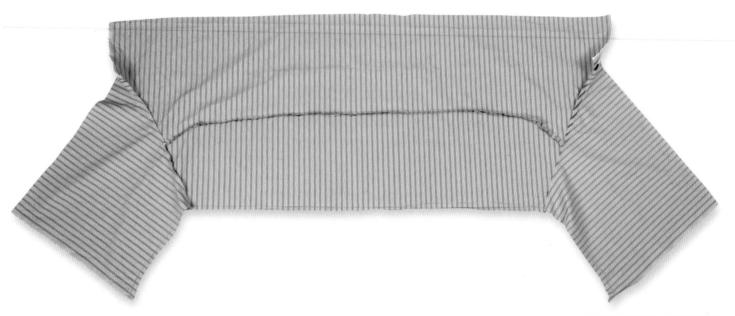

▲ 55. The covering fabric for the back rest is positioned. Measure its dimensions (see page 70) and cut two pieces which will constitute its central section; then they are united to form a small seam allowance at the rear section. This seam coincides with the furrow and the strap will be used to sew the fabric to the back rest. The pieces that will cover the arm rests are also measured and cut, and then sewn to the central piece. Both pieces have to be perfectly symmetrical as does the seam, so that the seams of both pieces will be equidistant to the center of the back rest and positioned similarly.

▶ 56. To attach the back rest fabric it will be necessary to add a strip which will be stapled to the frame of the sofa. A strawberry-colored piping is sewn to the lower part of the piece, making up the lower finishing of the back rest upholstery. The piping will not be seen, but is functional. Under the piping, an extra piece of fabric, called a "stretcher," is attached to pull and secure the inside back snugly.

◄ **57.** The stretcher is sewn over the line of the piping seam. Note that the center of the fabric has been marked with a small cut at the edge.

▼ **58.** The piece is placed on the back rest and centered with the help of the previous mark at the seat front. The lines have to be perfectly straight and aligned and must correspond to those on the seat. The assembly is held together with skewers.

► **59.** Now the stretcher is passed below the back rest (see steps 42 and 43), which has received a few cuts for the mounting frame, and is affixed with skewers. The skewers are removed from the top section of the back rest and the strip that unites the two pieces is attached to the central furrow with skewers.

► **60.** The sofa is turned so the back rest lies horizontally on top of the sawhorses, and the seam allowance is sewn to the back rest with the top stitch using a double-pointed needle and strawberry-colored jute thread matching the fabric.

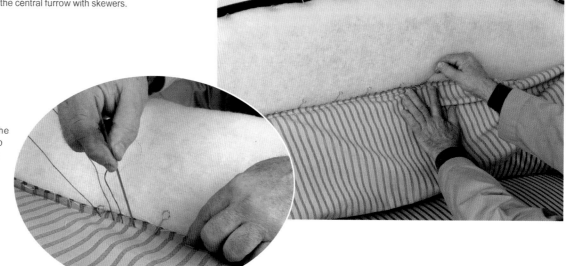

▶ **61.** The top stitch allows for a deep stitch which will result in a marked furrow. Pull the thread evenly while stitching so the seam is perfectly smooth.

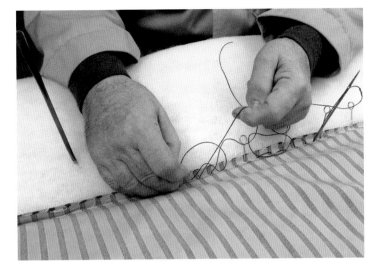

▼ **62.** The fabric is affixed to the top section of the back rest with tacks, proceeding from the center to the sides.

▲ **63.** View of the attached fabric of the back rest. Note that the strawberry-colored piping is at the lower section, functioning as a finish between the back rest and the seat. The lines of the upholstery of both parts should match each other and be perfectly straight.

▲ **64.** Then the arm rest area is attached. First a cut parallel to the top frame of the seat is made up to the arm rest.

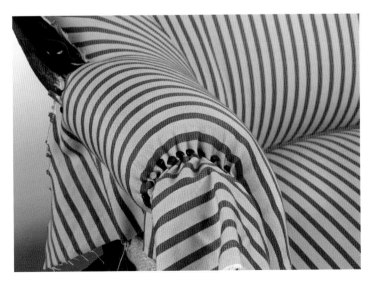

◀ **65.** Cutting the fabric has exposed the frame from the back rest up to the arm rest. Avoid making a cut that is too long. The fabric is pulled and tacked to the arm rests. The front side of the arm rest receives numerous tacks to achieve the desired curvature.

▼ **66.** The rear section is also cut; avoid ripping the fabric.

133

► **67.** At this point the entire fabric covering is stapled and the extra fabric is cut off. The straps of the back rest that were created by cutting into the stretcher piece are affixed to the frame of the seat with staples, and again the extra fabric is cut off.

▼ **68.** To make the rear section, sturdy white fabric is stapled to the frame.

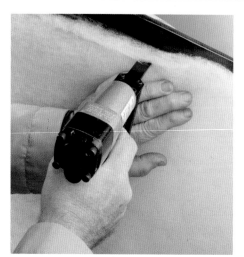

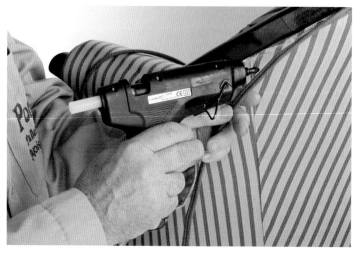

▲ **69.** A piece of batting of density 300 is affixed to it, perfectly tensioned, and is stapled to the frame. The extra fabric is cut off.

▲ **70.** For the upholstering of the back rest proceed as with the front part of the seat: cut a piece for the center, and sew the pieces that form the sides to it. The stripes have to be perfectly straight, and the horizontal ones should match those of the arm rest. The upholstery is finished with a strawberry-colored double piping attached with a glue gun.

▼ **71.** The finished sofa.

Headboard

This project shows the process of creating a tufted headboard of 5' 3" by 31¹/₂" (160 by 80 cm) for a bed that is 59" (150 cm) wide. The process includes the construction of the frame for its base, the filling, creating the template and distribution of the tufting, and making the buttons, as well as the finishing of both sides. Polyurethane foam and batting are used for the filling, while high-quality full-grain leather is used for the exterior covering. This headboard contains built-in reading lamps, so it will be necessary to make some boxes to accommodate them.

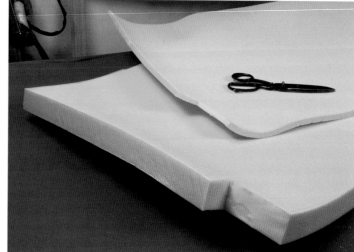

◀ **1.** A frame was made of 2-by-2 lumber (55 x 55 mm). It includes boxes at the top front of the headboard where the lights will be mounted.

▶ **2.** To prepare the filling for the headboard, the interior dimensions of the frame are marked on a 2-inch-thick (5 cm) piece of polyurethane foam of firm density.

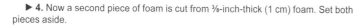

▲ **3.** Use a cutter to cut along the lines.

▶ **4.** Now a second piece of foam is cut from ⅜-inch-thick (1 cm) foam. Set both pieces aside.

► **5.** Next the burlap is positioned; it will form the base of the webbing assembly. In this case a coffee sack made from jute fiber is used. It is affixed with ½-inch-wide, ½-inch-long (13 mm) staples (80/380) to the back side of the rear section of the frame, perfectly tensioned.

▼ **6.** The fabric is cut to leave the lamps' boxes unobstructed and the edge is stapled. Note that a hole has been drilled into the side of the frame for the necks of the lamps.

► **7.** Now the steel mounting plates for the back side are measured and marked 7⅞ inches (20 cm) in from the sides of the frame. A chisel is used to cut out the section for the hook to pass through to attach the headboard to the wall.

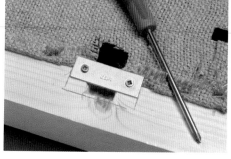

▲ **8.** Each plate is attached to the wood with two screws.

▲ **9.** The webbing is attached to the burlap fabric. In this case, the webbing is 3⅛-inch-wide (8 cm) jute. Measure and mark the centers of the two long sides of the frame and attach the first piece of webbing; first it is tensioned with the tensioning tool and then it is stapled with staples of similar size as before.

▲ **10.** After measuring the distance between the plates, four pieces of webbing are placed on each side, separated from each other by 2 inches (5 cm). Starting from the center piece of webbing, affix each one. Measure and adjust their placement before stapling them.

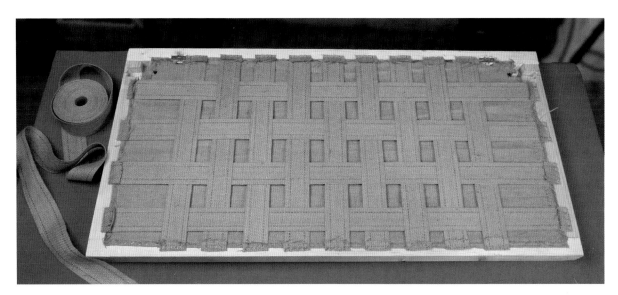

◀ **11.** Then four horizontal pieces of webbing are attached to the vertical sides of the frame, separated from each other by about 3⅛ inches (8 cm) and interwoven with the other webbing strips.

▶ **12.** The frame is turned front side up. Spray glue is applied to the burlap holding the can about 6 inches (15 cm) away from its surface, and the ⅜-inch-thick (1 cm) polyurethane foam piece is positioned.

▼ **13.** The foam is firmly pressed with both hands.

▲ **14.** Now the template for the tufting is made. Due to the dimensions of the headboard a diamond pattern of 4 ⁵⁄₁₆ x 5 ⅛ inches (11 x 13 cm) has been chosen. The 2-inch-thick (5 cm) piece of foam is placed into the frame and the precise center is measured and marked with a tape measure and a square so as to be perfectly aligned with the sides and perpendicular to the base and the upper edge. The width of the diamonds (4⁵⁄₁₆ inches / 11 cm) is marked with a pencil on the fronts of the long sides of the frame.

▲ **15.** Proceed the same way with the shorter sides: the first mark is made 2¹⁵⁄₁₆ inches (7.5 cm) from the outside top edge of the frame and the rest of the marks are about 5⅛ inches (13 cm) apart. The pencil marks are connected with a pencil using a long metal ruler; then mark the lines on the foam with a permanent marker.

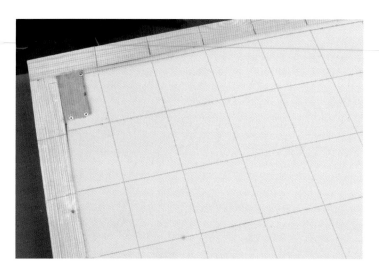

▲ **16.** The lines of the upper and lower sides are also extended; the result is the grid pattern base for the tufting.

▶ **17.** The template for the diamonds is created by extending the diagonals of the rectangles of the grid. The diagonals are traced first in one direction and then in the other.

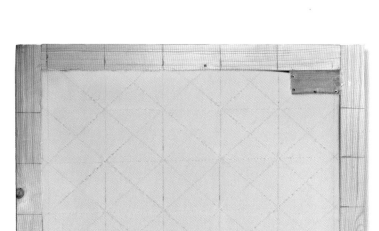

◀ **18.** The result is a grid-patterned base where the intersections of the diagonals mark the location of the buttons of the tufting.

▲ **19.** The thicker piece of foam is removed from the frame and placed on the work bench. The holes at the diagonals' intersections are made with a #12 punch iron. The foam should be placed on a piece of wood (in this case plywood) and the punch must be hammered perfectly vertical.

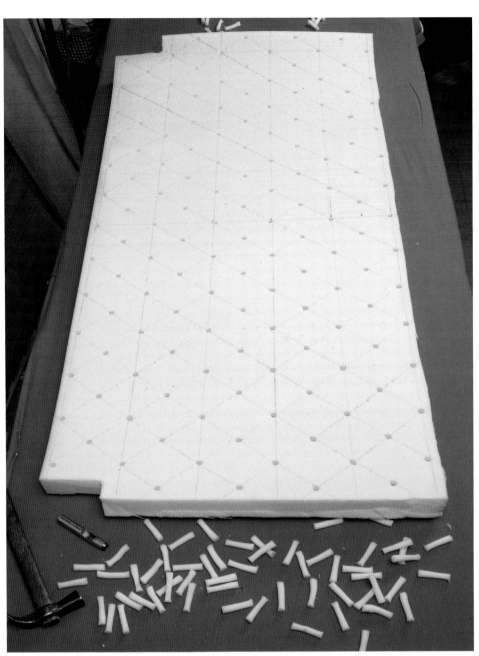

▶ **20.** The finished piece of foam, with the holes where the thread for the buttons will pass through.

▲ **21.** Next the punched piece is placed onto a piece of ¾-inch-thick (2-cm) foam. The new piece is larger and will be cut to size later. The holes of the upper piece are marked onto the lower with a permanent marker, with the upper piece acting as a template.

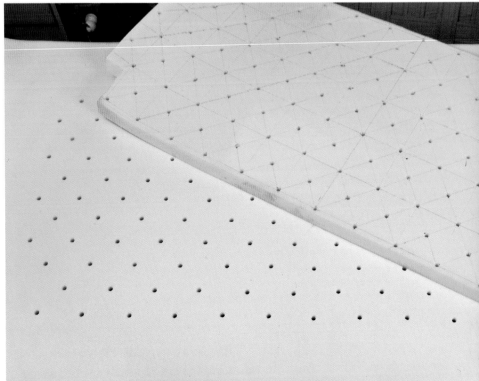

▶ **22.** Following the above method the piece of ¾-inch-thick (2-cm) foam is punched as well.

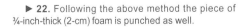

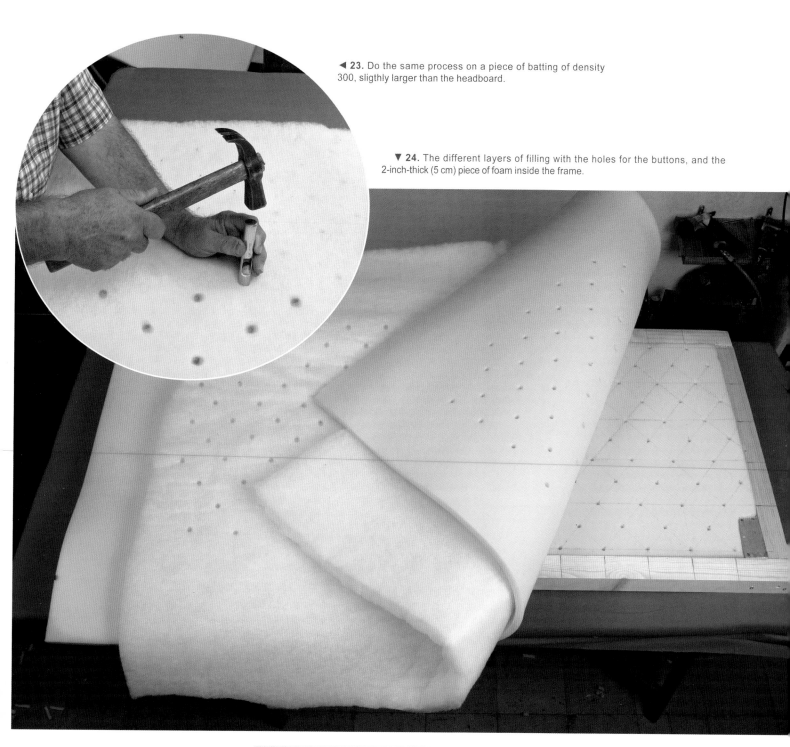

◄ **23.** Do the same process on a piece of batting of density 300, sligthly larger than the headboard.

▼ **24.** The different layers of filling with the holes for the buttons, and the 2-inch-thick (5 cm) piece of foam inside the frame.

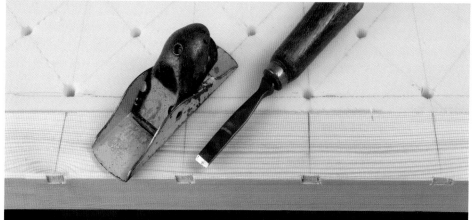

► **25.** The front edges of the frame are marked with a chisel. Due to the fact that the headboard will be upholstered with leather, a chisel will be used to cut out the four sides of the frame where the folds will be located (at the markings) to prevent them from sticking out from the headboard's surface.

► **26.** In order to work comfortably the frame is placed onto sawhorses for access to the back side later on. Now the piece of foam that will be the top part of the filling is cut about ⅔ inch (1.5 cm) larger than the outide dimensions of the frame, and is perfectly centered on it, matching up the holes. Apply contact glue to the front edge of the frame, separating the foam with a wooden support stick to prevent it from touching the adhesive.

▼ **27.** Also apply glue to the top section of the edge of the foam piece. Note that the wooden brace remains under it to separate it from the frame; this facilitates the task because it leaves both hands free.

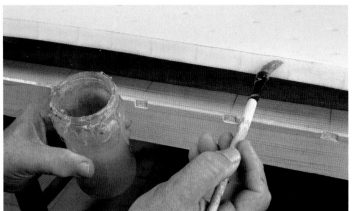

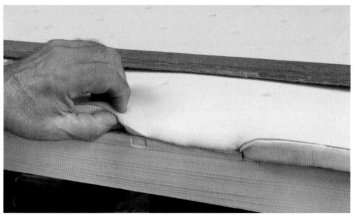

▲ **28.** After 10 to 15 minutes the brace is removed and the piece is glued to the front face of the frame, along the outer edge, while turning it so that the area with glue remains in contact with the wood. The gluing is done from the center progressing toward both edges at the same time.

◄ **29.** Proceed likewise with all sides. View of the piece affixed to the frame.

▶ **30.** The piece of batting is placed onto the assembly so that the holes match up to those in the foam. The placement of the batting is done using your sense of touch by reaching down to the bottom layer of foam and then aligning pieces of wood, in this case several long pencils.

▼ **31.** Now the jute twine used to sew the buttons is cut, to a length allowing each button's strand to be about 2½ feet (75 cm) long. It is helpful to use the length of your arm: one turn will result in the right length. Make as many loops as buttons to be sewn, and cut it at the end.

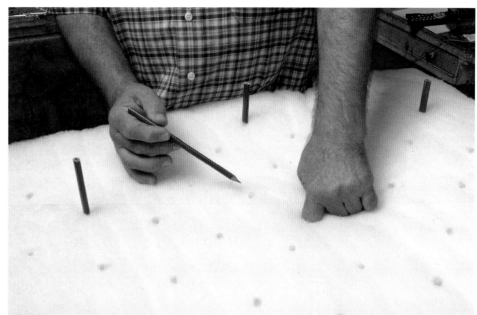

▲ **32.** The batting is attached to the frame with staples and then the threads are passed through. Thread the sewing needle leaving one end longer than the other, and pass it through the hole.

◀ **33.** The needle reaches to the back section of the headboard making a stitch about one finger's width wide. Then the needle is returned upward with the top end of the needle pointing up, passing through the hole.

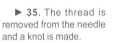

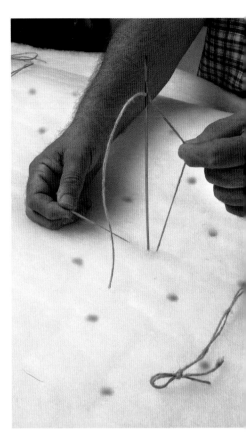

◄ 34. The needle is removed without letting go of the part of the thread which has been left at the top.

► 35. The thread is removed from the needle and a knot is made.

◄ 36. The same process is continued on the remaining holes of the headboard. The extra batting is cut off at both sides.

► 37. Then the placement of the tufting is marked on the wrong side of the leather. A sufficiently large piece has been selected to cover the entire surface of the headboard and to make the edges and other elements (buttons). It is important to leave an area of ⁹⁄₁₆ inch (1.5 cm) at each side of the diamond to make the folds of the tuft, therefore the piece must be at least 45¹¹⁄₁₆ x 89 inches (116 x 226 cm). It is placed onto the work bench with the wrong side up, it is measured, and the centers of both sides are marked with a ruler and a pencil. The measurements of the two lines of the diamonds are marked: 5½ inches wide x 6⁵⁄₁₆ inches high (14 x 16 cm).

▶ **38.** Two lines are traced perfectly parallel to the horizontal and the measurements of the width and the diagonals of the diamonds is marked on them.

▼ **39.** The height of the diamonds is marked likewise. Great attention must be paid when realizing the markings with the respective checks. The result is a grid of diamonds of 5½ x 6⁵⁄₁₆ inches (14 x 16 cm); the intersections mark where the buttons will be sewn.

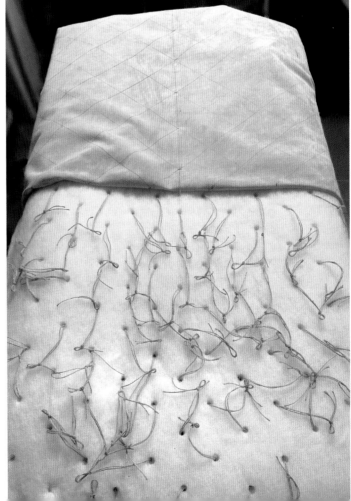

▶ **40.** The central hole of the base is marked and affixed with a skewer. Then the leather is placed centered on it so that its center coincides with the skewer and so it is perfectly aligned with respect to the vertical and horizontal axes of the frame. Check that the diagonals of the leather match the holes of the headboard—although they will not coincide perfectly because the diamonds marked on the leather are larger in order to accommodate the folds.

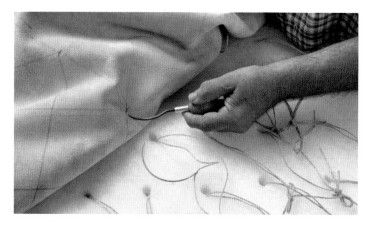

▲ **41.** Now the stitching of the leather is done starting from the central hole of the headboard. An awl is used to make the holes in the leather, which are separated by about ⁹⁄₁₆ inch (1.5 cm). The stitch is done this way in order to manage the leather appropriately. It is not advisable to leave a smaller separation.

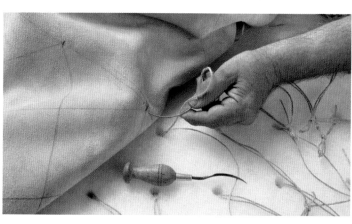

▲ **42.** Each end of the thread is passed with a circular needle through the holes.

▼ **43.** The thread is held with one hand and one of the ends is passed around the other with two turns to make the knot. Note the distance of ⁹⁄₁₆ inch (1.5 cm) between the threads.

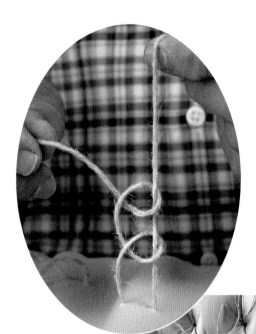

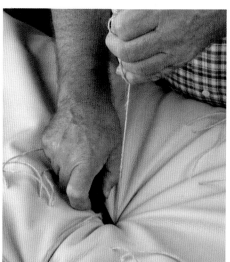

▲ **44.** Then firmly pull on the straight end of the thread while pressing with a rounded wooden stick onto the knot. The knot is now secured.

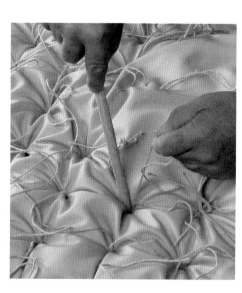

▲ **45.** Working by area, first the knots are knotted and the folds are made on one side, and then on the other.

► **46.** The regulator tool is used during the entire process.

◀ **47.** Once the knotting has been done the lateral folds of the tufting are made and affixed. They are measured to make sure they are perfectly aligned and equidistant from each other, some 4⁵/₁₆ inches (11 cm). Those at the lower and upper part of the headboard are made folded toward the same direction, while those of the sides are folded downward. They are affixed temporarily using tacks.

▼ **48.** General view of the knotted headboard with the temporarily-secured lateral folds.

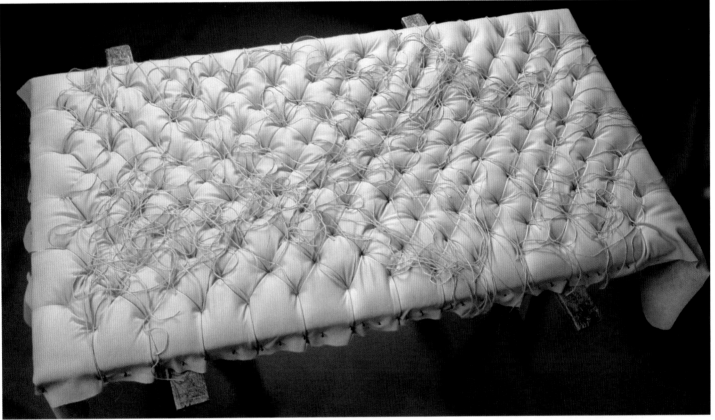

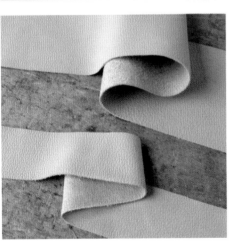

◀ **49.** Now the buttons are made. The chosen leather is too thick to use for this, so it must be pared thinner, either at the workshop itself or at a specialized leatherworking shop. The thickness is reduced to half. Note that the top piece has the original thickness; the lower piece is a pared-down piece of leather.

▶ **50.** The buttons are made with pieces of size 20 (see page 67). A few extra buttons are made so as to be able to replace them later if required, and to have enough buttons during the process.

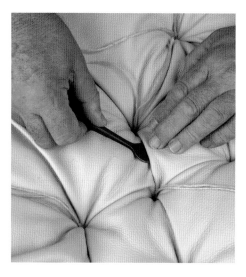

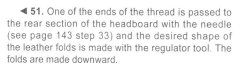

◄ 51. One of the ends of the thread is passed to the rear section of the headboard with the needle (see page 143 step 33) and the desired shape of the leather folds is made with the regulator tool. The folds are made downward.

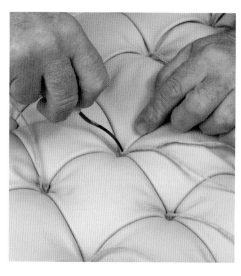

► 52. Now the buttons are sewn. A hole is made with the awl where the button will be sewn.

► 53. View of the rear while sewing the buttons. The two ends of the thread remain at the rear section of the headboard (see page 68).

▼ 54. With the headboard positioned from top to bottom on sawhorses, the threads of the buttons are knotted at the back. This process requires another person, with one pulling and knotting at the rear side and the other controlling the applied tension to position the buttons at the same depth.

► 55. The button-sewing process is complete.

► **56.** Now the sides are stapled with ½-inch-wide, ½-inch-long (13 mm) staples (80/380). The provisional tacks are removed with the tack puller and the extra fabric is cut off with a cutter.

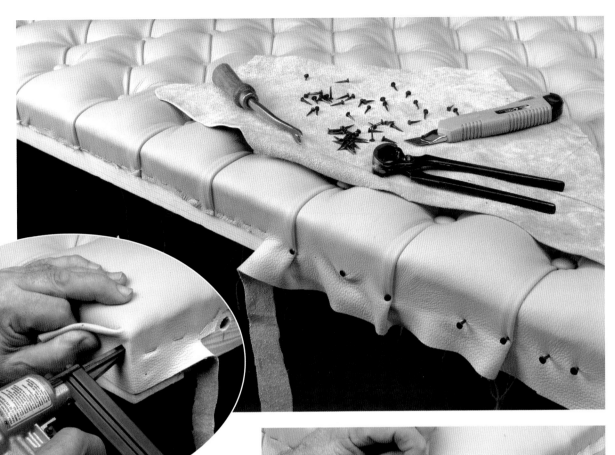

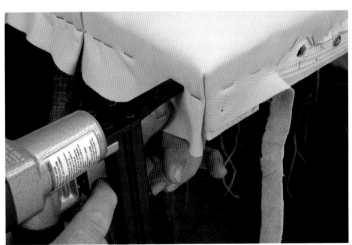

▲ **57.** The corners are trimmed with a fold. Because the leather is rather thick it is necessary to make a cut to keep the fold from being overly bulky. First the section of the fold that will be underneath is stapled.

► **58.** The fold is made and cut vertically with scissors.

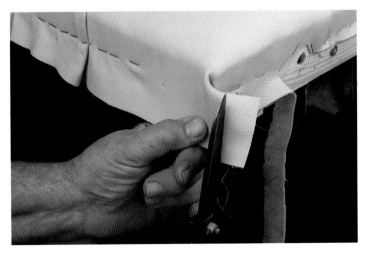

▲ **59.** The extra leather is also cut off and the final fold is made.

▲ **60.** Then it is stapled. Note that the sides of the headboard feature unobstructed holes to attach the lamps.

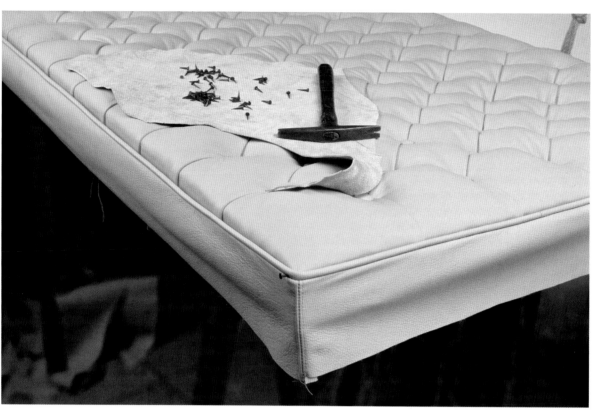

◄ **61.** The boxing piece covering the sides and the top is placed (see page 71) and affixed temporarily with tacks at the four corners. They are placed just below the piping to avoid marking the leather.

◄ **62.** It is affixed to the lower section of the frame, at the edge of the piping. To make sure that the piece is perfectly straight with respect to the surface of the headboard, measure before nailing and make sure that the union between the edge and the piping is 2³⁄₁₆ inches (5.5 cm) from the lower edge of the frame.

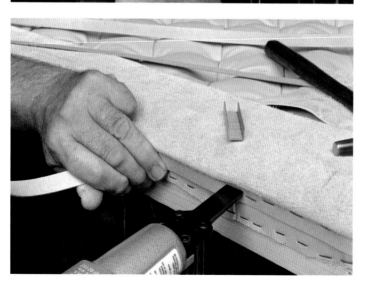

▲ **63.** Once checked, staple it using staples of similar size to the previous ones.

◄ **64.** Next a strip of 1-mm-thick cardboard is stapled over the area. The cardboard prevents the staples from protruding under the leather which could leave unsightly marks; at the same time it contributes to a clean line as the surface will be more even once the leather is pulled taut.

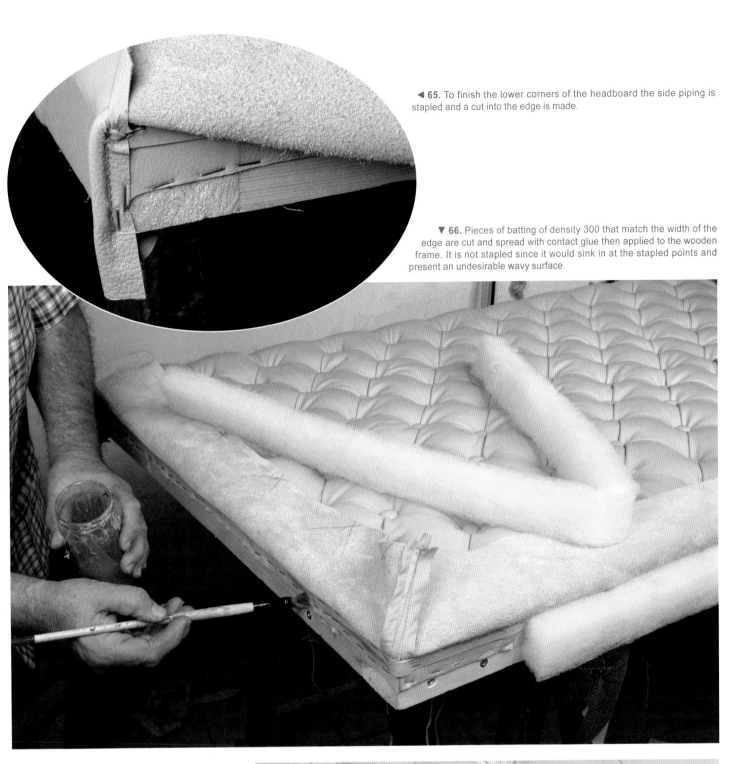

◄ 65. To finish the lower corners of the headboard the side piping is stapled and a cut into the edge is made.

▼ 66. Pieces of batting of density 300 that match the width of the edge are cut and spread with contact glue then applied to the wooden frame. It is not stapled since it would sink in at the stapled points and present an undesirable wavy surface.

► 67. The side is turned downward while smoothing and pulling it. It is then temporarily affixed with tacks. To prevent the batting from slipping it is placed centered with one hand while it is pulled with the other hand. It is permanently stapled with staples similar to the previous ones, and the extra fabric is cut off with scissors.

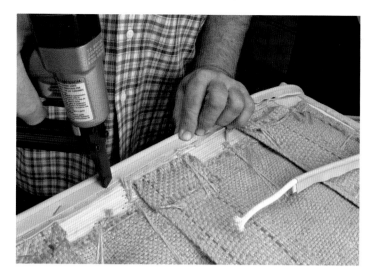

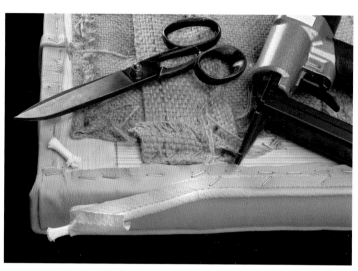

▲ **68.** To finish the section, piping is attached to the back of the long side. Note that some buttons have been knotted and affixed to the wooden frame by stapling their threads. This system is just as effective as the knotting and sewing shown previously, and it is much faster to execute.

▲ **69.** To finish the piping at the ends, you must unstitch a short length at the end and cut the inner core.

▲ **70.** It is turned sideways and stapled.

▶ **71.** Finally the rear section of the headboard is covered with white fabric which is attached with staples. The areas around the boxes for the lamps and cables are not attached. Holes are cut into the leather of the side piece where the arms of the lamps pass through.

▼ **72.** The finished headboard with the installed reading lamps.

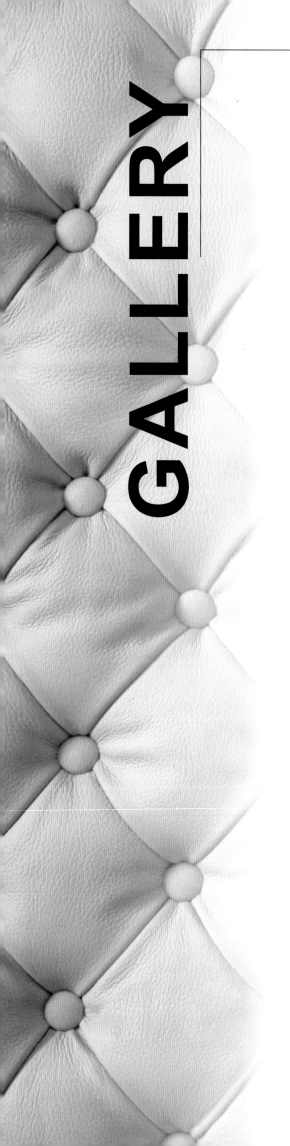

GALLERY

► Wingback chair and Stamford footrest. Wood frame and stained beechwood legs, tufted full-grain leather, bronze tacks. Chesterfields, Fleming & Howland, 2011.

▼ Gaudí-style chaise longue. Wood frame and fabric upholstery, golden legs and tacks with Swarovski crystals. Bretz, 2011.

► Isabel-style sofa, 19th century. Mahogany and traditional fabric upholstery. Tapicería Pons, 2005.

◄ Ludwig Mies van der Rohe, Barcelona® chair, 1929. Steel frame and contemporary padded upholstery with full-grain leather covering. KnollStudio®, Knoll, 2011.

► Harp mirror. Wood frame and Trevira CS®-covered upholstery, 6-mm-thick mirror glass, golden tacks. Bretz, 2011.

► Mamma armchair. Wood frame and leather upholstery with golden tacks. Bretz, 2011.

◄ Chaise longue. Wood frame with varnished visible section, fabric covering. Christopher Guy, 2011.

◄ Mammut table. Wood structure and Trevira CS® upholstery, 10-mm-thick glass. Bretz, 2011.

► Captain-style office chair. Mahogany wood and tufted upholstery with full-grain leather, bronze tacks, and wheels. Chesterfields, Fleming & Howland, 2011.

◄ Chesterfield sofa. Traditional upholstery with tufted back rest and full-grain leather covering. Tapicería Pons, 2011.

▲ Chaise longue. Traditional upholstery with velvet covering. Tapicería Pons, 2010.

▲ Dining room chair. Wood frame and varnished legs with fabric covering. Christopher Guy, 2011.

◄ Boudoir chair. Traditional tufted upholstery with velvet covering. Tapicería Pons, 2008.

▼ Armchair, England, 17th century. Walnut with Brussels tapestry covering finished with brass tacks.

► Window seat bench. Mahogany wood and tufted upholstery with full-grain leather covering, bronze tacks. Chesterfields, Fleming & Howland, 2011.

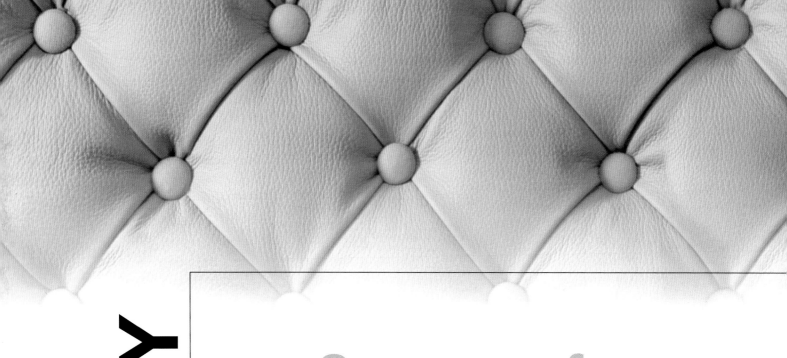

GLOSSARY

a

Awl. Tool for working with leather, consisting of a handle with a long and thin metal point with several facets. It is used to perforate and to make cuts.

c

Comfort seat. Type of complex seat where the springs which make up the front line are affixed to the wooden structure with metal fasteners while the rest is placed onto the webbing, same as with the fixed seat. The spring set requires a complex tying of the springs as well as creating a top ring to affix and to compress the general structure of the seat. The result is that the seat sinks independently of the frame when sitting down, being more flat than the fixed seat.

Cord. Used to mold the filling creating pronounced rounded trim, mostly on arm and back rests.

d

Double-pointed needle. Long needle with two points but with only one eye, mostly used to stitch filling with a top stitch.

Drop stitch. Used to provide consistency and to affix the filling toward the front, depending on the task. The stitches remain inside, so the stitch is invisible from the outside.

f

Fixed seat/crowned seat. Made on a base of webbing on which the springs are affixed; the springs are themselves tied directly to the top structure of the seat so that the spring set remains inside its frame. They are the most common style of seat, both in antique and contemporary furniture.

Frame. Structure or skeleton of the furniture or the object which is to be upholstered. The frame determines the type and the characteristics of the upholstery.

Frame also is the term for an independent structure that can be removed from the seat or the back rest of the piece of furniture and which, once upholstered, is affixed to its structure.

h

Hoop. Elongated piece of sheet metal that is used to pass through and weave cane.

Horsehair. Long hair from the mane, used as filling for traditional upholstery.

p

Padding. Generic term for simple padding which results in a simple shape. Not to be confused with tufted padding, a high-quality technique which is much more elaborate and complex.

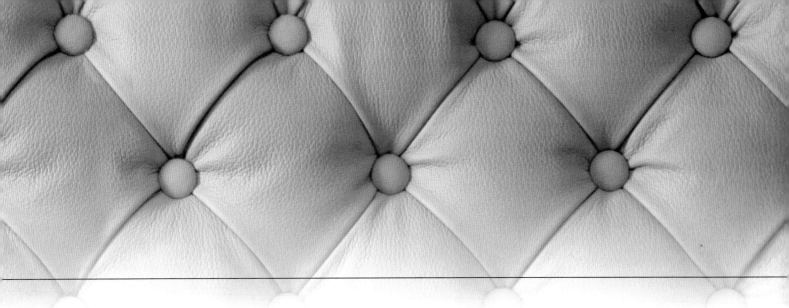

Paring (of leather). Thinning leather with a paring knife or machine. The machine consists of a special rasp which is applied to the flesh side to achieve the desired thickness.

Piping. Strip with a round profile, used to trim upholstery. Also known as welting or cording.

l

Ladder stitch. Parallel stitches which are similar to the rungs of a ladder. It is used to shape and affix the edges or contours of seats.

r

Rattan. Tropical plant from which stems and cores are extracted and used to make canework back rests and seats.

Regulator. Tool consisting of a steel or iron bar with one pointed end and the other shaped like a blade: broad, flat and thick. It is used to adjust the filling with the pointed end, and to adjust the folds of the covering with the flat end.

s

Single seat. This is the most simple type, made from a base consisting of webbing with a filling of horsehair or other materials and batting.

Skewer. A long thick needle with one pointed end and the other end curved like a ring, used for stitching processes and to temporarily hold fabrics and filling in place.

Staple. A U-shaped piece of steel with pointed ends. Used to affix springs and wires to the wooden frame.

Strap. Piece of fabric that is sewn to the covering when it is not long enough to be affixed to the frame. The strap increases the length of the covering and allows for a simple and secure attachment to the structure.

t

Tack puller. Tool consisting of a steel bar with a curved point ending in a claw. It is used to dismantle or remove upholstery, tacks, studs, and staples.

Tacks. Short nails used for temporary holding; or decorative studs used for finishing or trimming upholstery. The latter have larger heads and different shapes, profiles, and finishes.

Tie/bond. Long stitches (bridle stitches) made on the burlap of the upholstery. They are used to position and affix the filling.

Top stitch. Used to affix the top burlap by sewing it with the simple stitch to the lower burlap with the double-pointed needle.

Tufted. Derived from French, denoting upholstery with a cushioned filling which is affixed with buttons forming a regular and pronounced pattern. Not to be confused with padding, a much more simple and basic technique.

u

Upholsterer's needle. A semicircular needle with a round profile. Used to sew various items in upholstery.

W

Wadding. Unwoven polyester or cotton fiber fabric that is used as the final layer of upholstery filling.

Webbing. Strips of jute that are affixed to the frame and make up the base of the upholstery.

Webbing stretcher. Tool used to stretch webbing. The most common model consists of a handle with one rounded end which is covered with a nailed piece of rubber or leather. This tool can can be made in the workshop.

BIBLIOGRAPHY

AND ACKNOWLEDGMENTS

Dobson, Cherry. *The Complete Guide to Upholstery: Stuffed with Step-by-Step Techniques for Professional Results.* St. Martin's Griffin, New York, 2009.

Gates, Dorothy. *Guía esencial del tapizado.* Edimat, Madrid, 2005.

LaHalle, Charlotte. *Cannage. Rempaillage.* Éditions Fleurus, París, 2001.

Luke, Heather. *Easy Upholstery.* Krause Publications, Iola, WI, 1994.

The authors would like to thank Parramón Ediciones and in particular Tomàs Ubach for his trust in us to accomplish this project. We particularly want to thank Joan Soto for his tremendous assistance and professionalism. Also, Natàlia Guillamet; without her help this book would not be a reality.

We would also like to thank the companies, individuals, and professionals who have collaborated in the making of this book and who have made it possible, especially:

Enrique Arizón Guillot
Alicia Bas
Anna Bosch
Montserrat Cuadras
Neus Clofent
Alicia Jorge
Ramon Manent
Aina Pascual
Yolanda Pons
The Pou family
The Puig–Fernández family
Sr. Sol Muntañola

Associació Arapdis
www.artsana.cat

Associació per a l'Estudi del Moble
www.estudidelmoble.com

Arredamento Lombardo s.p.a.
www.arlom.com

Aura Fabrics
www.aurafabrics.com

Bretz Wohnträume GmbH
www.bretz.de

Decortex Firenze S.p.a
www.decortex.com

Emedemar, S.L.
juancarlosgavalda@yahoo.es

Fleming & Howland
www.chesterfields1780.com

Christopher Guy
www.christopherguy.com

Knoll, Inc.
www.knoll.com

Ramon Manent
www.photos-art.com

NOHO Modern
www.nohomodern.com

Tapicería Pons
www.tapiceriapons.es

Taycor, S.A.
taycor@taycor.e.telefonica.net

Vint-trenta
www.vinttrenta.com